WHERE DOES MONEY COME FROM?

A GUIDE TO THE UK MONETARY AND BANKING SYSTEM

JOSH RYAN-COLLINS, TONY GREENHAM, RICHARD WERNER AND ANDREW JACKSON

FOREWORD BY CHARLES A. E. GOODHART

nef (new economics foundation)

ACKNOWLEDGEMENTS

The authors would like to thank Ben Dyson for his valuable contributions to the writing of this book.

We are also most grateful to Professor Victoria Chick, Jon Relleen, James Meadway, Professor Charles Goodhart, Mark Burton and Sue Charman for their helpful insights and comments.

We are indebted to Elli Moody and John Jackson for their fortitude and patience in the design, editing and production of the book in the face of our late amendments.

Finally, we would like to express our gratitude to James Bruges and Marion Wells, without whom the book would not have been written.

That said, the contents of this book, and any mistakes or omissions, remain entirely the responsibility of the authors.

CONTENTS

FOREWORD

Far from money being 'the root of all evil', our economic system cannot cope without it. Hence the shock-horror when the Lehman failure raised the spectre of an implosion of our banking system. It is far nearer the truth to claim that 'Evil is the root of all money', a witty phrase coined by Nobu Kiyotaki and John Moore. If we all always paid our bills in full with absolute certainty, then everyone could buy anything on his/her own credit, by issuing an IOU on him/herself.

Since that happy state of affairs is impossible, (though assumed in most standard macro-models – to their detriment), we use as money the short-term ('sight') claim on the most reliable (powerful) debtor. Initially, of course, this powerful debtor was the State; note how the value of State money collapses when the sovereign power is overthrown. Coins are rarely full-bodied, and even then need guaranteeing by the stamp of the ruler seigniorage.

But there were severe disadvantages in relying solely on the government to provide sufficient money for everyone to use; perhaps most importantly, people could not generally borrow from the government. So, over time, we turned to a set of financial intermediaries, the banks, to provide us both with an essential source of credit and a reliable, and generally safe and acceptable, monetary asset.

Such deposit money was reliable and safe, because all depositors reckoned that they could always exchange their sight deposits with banks on demand into legal tender. This depended on the banks themselves having full access to legal tender, and again over time, central banks came to have monopoly control over such base money. So, the early analysis of the supply of money focussed on the relationship between the supply of base money created by the central bank and the provision by commercial banks of both bank credit and bank deposits, the bank multiplier analysis.

But, in practice, the central bank has always sought to control the level of interest rates, rather than the monetary base. Hence, as Richard Werner and his co-authors Josh Ryan-Collins, Tony Greenham and Andrew Jackson document so clearly in this book, the supply of money is actually determined primarily by the demand of borrowers to take out bank loans. Moreover, when such demand is low, because the economy is weak and hence interest rates are also driven down to zero, the relationship between available bank reserves (deposits at the central bank) and commercial bank lending/deposits can break down entirely. Flooding banks with additional liquidity, as central banks have done recently via Quantitative Easing (QE), has not led to much commensurate increase in bank lending or broad money.

All this is set out in nice detail in this book, which will provide the reader with a clear path through the complex thickets of misunderstandings of this important issue. In addition the authors provide many further insights into current practices of money and banking. At a time when we face up to massive challenges in financial reform and regulation, it is essential to have a proper, good understanding of how the monetary system works, in order to reach better alternatives. This book is an excellent guide, and will be suitable for a wide range of audiences, including not only those new to the field but also to policy-makers and academics.

Charles A. E. Goodhart
Professor Emeritus of Banking and Finance,
London School of Economics

19th September 2011

Overview

There is widespread misunderstanding of how new money is created. This book examines the workings of the UK monetary system and concludes that the most useful description is that new money is created by commercial banks when they create credit, either through making loans, buying existing assets or when customers draw down on their overdrafts. In creating credit, banks simultaneously create deposits in our bank accounts, which, to all intents and purposes, is money.

Many people would be surprised to learn that even among bankers, economists, and policymakers, there is no common understanding of how new money is created. This is a problem for two main reasons. First, in the absence of this understanding, attempts at banking reform are more likely to fail. Second, the creation of new money and the allocation of purchasing power are a vital economic function and highly profitable. This is therefore a matter of significant public interest and not an obscure technocratic debate. Greater clarity and transparency about this could improve both the democratic legitimacy of the banking system and our economic prospects.

Defining money is surprisingly difficult. We cut through the tangled historical and theoretical debate to identify that anything widely accepted as payment, particularly by the government as payment of tax, is, to all intents and purpose, money. This includes bank credit because although an IOU from a friend is not acceptable at the tax office or in the local shop, an IOU from a bank most definitely is.

We identify that the UK's national currency exists in three main forms, the second two of which exist in electronic form:

1. Cash – banknotes and coins.

2. Central bank reserves – reserves held by commercial banks at the Bank of England.

3. Commercial bank money – bank deposits created either when commercial banks lend money, thereby crediting credit borrowers' deposit accounts, make payments on behalf of customers using their overdraft facilities, or when they purchase assets from the private sector and make payments on their own account (such as salary or bonus payments).

Only the Bank of England or the government can create the first two forms of money, which is referred to in this book as 'central bank money'. Since central bank reserves do not actually circulate in the economy, we can further narrow down the money supply that is actually circulating as consisting of cash and commercial bank money.

Physical cash accounts for less than 3 per cent of the total stock of money in the economy. Commercial bank money – credit and coexistent deposits – makes up the remaining 97 per cent of the money supply.

There are several conflicting ways of describing what banks do. The simplest version is that banks take in money from savers, and lend this money out to borrowers. This is not at all how the process works. Banks do not need to wait for a customer to deposit money before they can make a new loan to someone else. In fact, it is exactly the opposite; the making of a loan creates a new deposit in the customer's account.

More sophisticated versions bring in the concept of 'fractional reserve banking'. This description recognises that banks can lend out many times more than the amount of cash and reserves they hold at the Bank of England. This is a more accurate picture, but is still incomplete and misleading. It implies a strong link between the amount of money that banks create and the amount that they hold at the central bank. It is also commonly assumed by this approach that the central bank has significant control over the amount of reserves banks hold with it.

We find that the most accurate description is that banks create new money whenever they extend credit, buy existing assets or make payments on their own account, which mostly involves expanding their assets, and that their ability to do this is only very weakly linked to the amount of reserves they hold at the central bank. At the time of the financial crisis, for example, banks held just £1.25 in reserves for every £100 issued as credit. Banks operate within an electronic clearing system that nets out multilateral payments at the end of each day, requiring them to hold only a tiny proportion of central bank money to meet their payment requirements.

The power of commercial banks to create new money has many important implications for economic prosperity and financial stability. We highlight four that are relevant to the reforms of the banking system under discussion at the time of writing:

1. Although useful in other ways, capital adequacy requirements have not and do not constrain money creation, and therefore do not necessarily serve to

restrict the expansion of banks' balance sheets in aggregate. In other words, they are mainly ineffective in preventing credit booms and their associated asset price bubbles.

2. Credit is rationed by banks, and the primary determinant of how much they lend is not interest rates, but confidence that the loan will be repaid and confidence in the liquidity and solvency of other banks and the system as a whole.

3. Banks decide where to allocate credit in the economy. The incentives that they face often lead them to favour lending against collateral, or assets, rather than lending for investment in production. As a result, new money is often more likely to be channelled into property and financial speculation than to small businesses and manufacturing, with profound economic consequences for society.

4. Fiscal policy does not in itself result in an expansion of the money supply. Indeed, the government has in practice no direct involvement in the money creation and allocation process. This is little known, but has an important impact on the effectiveness of fiscal policy and the role of the government in the economy.

The basic analysis of this book is neither radical nor new. In fact, central banks around the world support the same description of where new money comes from. And yet many naturally resist the notion that private banks can really create money by simply making an entry in a ledger. Economist J. K. Galbraith suggested why this might be:

> *The process by which banks create money is so simple that the mind is repelled. When something so important is involved, a deeper mystery seems only decent.*[1]

This book aims to firmly establish a common understanding that commercial banks create new money. There is no deeper mystery, and we must not allow our mind to be repelled. Only then can we properly address the much more significant question: Of all the possible alternative ways in which we ***could*** create new money and allocate purchasing power, is this really the best?

I am afraid that the ordinary citizen will not like to be told that the banks or the Bank of England can create and destroy money.

Reginald McKenna, ex-Chancellor of the Exchequer, 1928[2]

I feel like someone who has been forcing his way through a confused jungle ... [A]lthough my field of study is one which is being lectured upon in every University in the world, there exists, extraordinarily enough, no printed Treatise in any language – so far I am aware – which deals systematically and thoroughly with the theory and facts of Representative Money as it exists in the modern world.

John Maynard Keynes, 1930[3]

INTRODUCTION

Money and banking are not only central to any modern economy, but their importance and prominence in the public eye have been magnified since the global financial crisis of 2008. Yet both the general public and many experts have hazy conceptions of money and of how money relates to banking. For example, in a survey of the British public carried out last year, 74 per cent of people believed that they were legal owners of the money in their current account.[4] In fact, as we shall see, people do not own this money; rather, the bank owes it to them. Furthermore, in economics textbooks and even in a report published by the Independent Commission on Banking in September 2011,[5] inaccurate descriptions of the bank lending process are still put forward.

We do not believe these misunderstandings are the result of a conspiracy by bankers, economists, and central bankers, as is sometimes suggested by those who seek reforms. Just because current arrangements might suit some of these parties in terms of power and wealth does not imply any lack of sincere belief in the integrity of the system as they understand it. Rather, we share the late J.K. Galbraith's and the very present Warren Mosler's conception of 'innocent fraud'. And herein lies the problem; until there is a common and correct understanding of money and banking, little progress will be made in ensuring that the system is safe and performs to the greatest benefit of society and economy.

This book is an attempt to forge a shared understanding of money and banking through a careful and precise analysis. The focus is a factual, objective review of how the system works in the United Kingdom, but it would be brave indeed of us to claim this as the complete and definitive account. Reaching a good understanding requires us to interpret the nature and history of money and banking, set out in Chapter 2, and these contain subjective elements by their very nature. Instead we hope to demonstrate that our account is the best fit with the empirical observations of the workings of the system as it operates today in the UK, as set out in the following chapters. This is descriptive in nature and is based on detailed research and consultation with experts, including from the Bank of England and ex-commercial bank staff. We hope that even where the readers take issue with our historical and conceptual account of money, they will nevertheless find this book a useful resource that will assist their own thinking.

Where does money come from?

Key questions

The financial crisis of 2008/2009 has raised many more questions about our national system of banking and money than it has answered. Along with questions around the crisis itself (Why did it happen? How can we prevent it happening again?), there has been some basic questioning of the nature of banks and money. These have included:

- Where did all that money come from? – in reference to the credit bubble.

- Where did the money all go? – in reference to the credit crunch.

- How did the government (via the Bank of England) suddenly create £200 billion of new money through 'quantitative easing'?

- Are there not cheaper and more efficient ways to manage a banking crisis than to burden taxpayers and precipitate cutbacks in public expenditure?

These questions are very important. They allude to a bigger question which is the main subject of this book: How is money created and allocated in the UK? This seems like a question that should have a simple answer. However, there is no clear answer in the public domain that is easily accessible to the public.

In this book we try throughout to keep explanations simple, using non-technical language and diagrams. We believe that it is possible to describe the role of money and banking in simpler terms than has generally been the case. A broader public understanding of the facts is a necessary condition for the success of serious reforms in this area and the functioning of the democratic process.

How the book is structured

This book is divided into six chapters. Chapter 1 reviews the popular conception of banks as financial intermediaries and custodians, examines and critiques the textbook 'money multiplier' model of credit creation and then provides a more accurate description of the money creation process.

Chapter 2 examines what we mean by 'money'. Without a proper understanding of money, we cannot attempt to understand banking. We disagree with the view of money as a commodity, often presented in mainstream economics and show instead that money is a social relationship of credit and debt. The second half of the chapter reviews the emergence of modern credit money in the UK, moving through fractional reserve banking, bond-issuance, the creation of a central bank, the Gold Standard and deregulation and the emergence of digital money in the late twentieth century.

Chapter 3 lays out how today's monetary system operates in simple steps. We define modern money through the notion of purchasing power and liquidity and then set out how the payment system works, the role of central bank reserves, interbank settlement and clearing, cash, deposit insurance and then the role of the central bank in influencing the money supply through monetary policy. We also examine the concept of bank 'solvency' and 'capital' and examine what a commercial bank's balance sheet looks like.

Chapter 4 lays out the role of government spending, borrowing, and taxation (fiscal policy) and international dimensions of the monetary system, including the constraints on money creation imposed by the European Union and how foreign exchange effects the monetary system. More detail is provided in Appendix 4.

Chapter 5 examines the extent to which commercial bank money is effectively regulated. We examine how the Bank of England attempts to conduct monetary policy through interventions in the money markets to move the price of money (interest rate), and via more direct dealings with banks. We also examine capital adequacy ratios as a tool for influencing credit creation. This section also includes a review of the financial crisis and how neither liquidity nor capital adequacy regulatory frameworks were effective in preventing asset bubbles and ultimately the crisis itself. Building on the theoretical analysis in Chapter 2, we argue the case for more direct intervention in credit markets and provide some international examples.

Finally, the conclusion summarises the argument and sets out a range of questions raised by the book. We hope to address these questions in later research. Before this can be done, however, a better and common general understanding of how the monetary system works is required.

1. What do banks do?

Our bankers are indeed nothing but Goldsmiths' shops where, if you lay money on demand, they allow you nothing; if at time, three per cent.'

Daniel Defoe, Essay on Projects, 1690[6]

It proved extraordinarily difficult for economists to recognize that bank loans and bank investments do create deposits.

Joseph Schumpeter, 1954[7]

1.1. The confusion around banking

There is significant confusion about banks. Much of the public is unclear about what banks actually do with their money. Economics graduates are slightly better informed, yet many textbooks used in undergraduate economics courses teach a model of banking that has not applied in the UK for a few decades, and unfortunately many policymakers and economists still work on this outdated model.

The confusion arises because the reality of modern banking is complex and partially hidden. In researching for this book, we had to piece together information that was spread across more than 500 documents, guides, manuals, and papers from central banks, regulators, and other authorities. Few economists have time to do this research firsthand and most individuals in the financial sector only have expertise in a small area of the system, meaning that there is a shortage of people who have a truly accurate and comprehensive understanding of the modern banking and monetary system as a whole. This section gives a brief overview of the common misconceptions about what banks do, and then gives an initial overview of what they actually do. A more detailed explanation is provided in Chapter 3.

1.2. Popular perceptions of banking 1: the safe-deposit box

Most people will have had a piggy bank at some point in their childhood. The idea is simple: keep putting small amounts of money into your piggy bank, and the money will just sit there safely until you need to spend it.

For many people, this idea of keeping money safe in some kind of box ready for a 'rainy day' persists into adult life. A poll conducted by ICM on behalf of the

Cobden Centre[8] found that 33 per cent of people were under the impression that a bank does not make use of the money in customers' current accounts. When told the reality – that banks don't just keep the money safe in the bank's vault but use it for other purposes – this group of people answered 'This is wrong – I have not given them my permission to do so.'

1.2.1. We do not own the money we have put in the bank

The custodial role that banks are assumed to play by a third of the public is something of an illusion. Similar confusion is found over the ownership of the money that we put into our bank accounts. The ICB/Cobden Centre poll found that 77 per cent of people believed that the money they deposited in banks legally belonged to them.[9] In fact, the money that they deposited legally belongs to the bank.

When a member of the public makes a deposit of £1,000 in the bank, the bank does not hold that money in a safe box with the customer's name on it (or any digital equivalent). Whilst banks do have cash vaults, the cash they keep there is not customers' money.

Instead, the bank takes legal ownership of the cash deposited and records that they owe the customer £1,000. In the accounting of the bank, this is recorded as a liability of the bank to the customer. It is liability because at some point in the future, it may have to be repaid.

The concept of a 'liability' is essential to understanding modern banking, and is actually very simple. If you were to borrow £50 from a friend, you might make a note in your diary to remind you to repay the £50 a couple of weeks later. In the language of accounting, this £50 is a liability of you to your friend.

The balance of your bank account, and indeed the bank account of all members of the public and all businesses, is the bank's IOU, and shows that they have a legal obligation (i.e. liability) to pay the money at some point in the future. (Whether they will actually have that money at the time you need it is a different issue, as we explain later.)

1.3. Popular perceptions of banking 2: taking money from savers and lending it to borrowers

The ICM/Cobden Centre poll found that around 61 per cent of the public share a slightly more accurate understanding of banking: the idea that banks take money from savers and lend it to borrowers. When asked if they were

Figure 1: Banks as financial intermediaries.[10]

concerned about this process, this group answered 'I don't mind as long as the banks pay interest and aren't too reckless.'

This view sees banks as financial intermediaries, recycling and allocating our savings into (we hope) profitable investments that provide us with a financial return in the form of interest. The interest we receive on savings accounts is an incentive to save and a form of compensation for not spending the money immediately. Banks give lower interest to savers than they charge to borrowers in order to make a profit and cover their losses in case of default. The difference between the interest rate banks pay to savers and the interest they charge to borrowers is called the 'interest rate spread' or 'margin'.

Banks intermediate money across space (savings in London may fund loans in Newcastle); and time (my savings are pooled with those of others and loaned over a longer-term period to enable a borrower to buy a house). Shifting money and capital around the economy, and transforming short-term savings into long-term loans (a process known as 'maturity transformation') is very important for the broader economy: it ensures that savings are actively being put to use by the rest of the economy rather than lying dormant under our mattresses. We can also invest our money directly with companies by purchasing shares or bonds issued by them. The process of saving and investment indirectly through banks, and directly to companies, is summarised in Figure 1.

> ## Box 1: Retail, commercial, wholesale, and investment banking
>
> Banking is commonly categorised according to the type of activities and the type of customers. In this book we use the generic term 'commercial banks' to refer to all non-state deposit-taking institutions, and to distinguish them from the central bank.
>
> However, commercial banking can also be used to describe the provision of services to larger companies. The Independent Commission on Banking sets out the following different categories of banking:[11]
>
> ### Retail and commercial banking
>
> The provision of deposit-taking, payment and lending services to retail customers and small and medium-sized enterprises (SMEs) (retail, or 'high-street' banking) and to larger companies (commercial banking).
>
> ### Wholesale and investment banking
>
> This involves the provision of wholesale lending to large corporations (wholesale banking) and the provision of assistance (including underwriting) to institutions such as governments and corporations in raising equity and debt finance, providing advice in relation to mergers and acquisitions, acting as counterparty to client trades and market-making (investment banking). An investment bank may also undertake trading on its own account (proprietary trading) in a variety of financial products (such as derivatives, fixed income instruments, currencies, and commodities).
>
> Note that investment banks need not necessarily hold a licence to accept deposits from customers to carry out some of these trading and advisory activities.

Banks, according to this viewpoint, are important, but relatively neutral, players in our financial system, almost like the lubricant that enables the cogs of consumption, saving, and production to turn smoothly. So it is perhaps understandable that orthodox economists do not put banks or money at the heart of their models of the economy. Maybe sometimes things go wrong – banks allocate too many savings to a particular industry sector for example that is prone to default – but in the long run, so the theory states, it is not the banks themselves that are really determining economic outcomes.

This theory is incorrect, for reasons that will be covered below. It also leads to assumptions about the economy that do not hold true in reality, such as the idea that high levels of savings by the public will lead to high investment in productive businesses (and conversely that a lack of savings by the public will choke off investment in productive businesses).

Most importantly, this understanding of banking completely overlooks the question: Where does money come from? Money is implicitly assumed to come from the Bank of England (after all, that's what it says on every £5 or

£10 note), the Royal Mint, or some other part of the state. The reality is quite different, as the rest of this chapter explains.

1.4. Three forms of money

At this point we need to clarify the different forms of money that we use in our economy.

The simplest form is **cash** – the £5, £10, £20, and £50 bank notes and the metal coins that most of us will have in our wallets at any point in time. Paper notes are created under the authority of the Bank of England (and printed by specialist printer De La Rue). Although cash is being used for fewer and fewer transactions, the fact that prices tend to rise and the population is growing means that the Bank of England expects the total amount of cash in circulation in the economy to keep growing over time.

Of course, we do not like having to ferry around huge sums of cash when making payments, as this is expensive and also runs the risk of theft or robbery. So instead, most payments for larger sums are made electronically. This raises the question of who creates and allocates electronic money or computer money. Not surprisingly, the Bank of England can create electronic money. It may do so, when granting a loan to its customers, allowing them to use a kind of 'overdraft' facility or when making payments to purchase assets or pay the salaries of its staff. The most important customers are the government and the commercial banks.

While many assume that only the Bank of England has the right to create computer money, in actual fact this accounts for only a tiny fraction of the money supply. The majority of the money supply – as mentioned – is electronic money created by commercial banks. How these (usually) private sector banks create and allocate the money supply remains little known to both the public and many trained economists, as it is not covered in most textbooks.

These first two types of money – cash and reserves – are collectively referred to as **central bank money**. Transactions between banks can either be settled bilaterally between themselves, or via their accounts with the central bank – where they hold what is known as **central bank reserves**. These central bank reserves are electronic money, are created by the Bank of England and are risk-free. However, unlike cash, members of the public cannot access or use central bank reserves. Only high-street and commercial banks that have accounts with the Bank of England are able to use this type of money.

Central bank reserves are used by banks for the settlement of interbank payments and liquidity management, further explained in Chapter 3.* The term 'money supply', usually refers to cash and commercial bank money. On the Bank of England's standard definition of the money supply, known as M4, cash makes up less than 3 per cent of the money supply.

The third type of money, however, is not created by the Bank of England, the Royal Mint, or any other part of government. This third type of money is what is in your bank account. In banking terminology, it's referred to as **bank deposits** or **demand deposits**. In technical terms, it is simply a number in a computer system; in accounting terms, it is a liability of the bank to you (what the banks owe you).

This is measured by the Bank of England's 'money supply' measures, ranging from M1 to M4. Such 'money supply' measures however often sow confusion, as they focus on banks' liabilities (deposits of the public with the banks). The reason is that not all deposits with banks were actually deposited by the public. As will be discussed below, when banks do what is commonly (and somewhat incorrectly) called 'lend money' or 'extend loans', they simply credit the borrower's deposit account and thus pretend that the borrowers have made deposits. This focus on bank deposits (and deposits with the central bank) distract from the money creation process, which takes place through credit creation (when banks lend or make payments, which can be gleaned from other parts of their balance sheet).

Bank deposits are not legal tender in the strict definition of the term – only coins and notes under certain conditions meet this test[†] – but as we will discuss, they function as money and most members of the public would consider them to be as good as cash. **It is this type of money that now makes up 97.4 per cent of all the money used in the economy.**[12] In this book we refer to the money created by banks as **commercial bank money**.

---

* 'Central bank money in the UK economy takes two forms: banknotes and banks' balances with the Bank of England (reserves). As a risk-free asset, reserves are used by banks for settlement of interbank payments and liquidity management'. Bank of England, *Red Book*, p.4.

† 'Legal tender has a very narrow and technical meaning in the settlement of debts. It means that a debtor cannot successfully be sued for non-payment if he pays into court in legal tender. It does not mean that any ordinary transaction has to take place in legal tender or only within the amount denominated by the legislation. Both parties are free to agree to accept any form of payment whether legal tender or otherwise according to their wishes.' Extract from the Royal Mint website. Retrieved from http://www.royalmint.com/corporate/policies/legal_tender_guidelines.aspx [accessed 9 August 2011].

1.5. How banks create money by extending credit

The vast majority of money in our economy was created by commercial banks. In effect what the UK, and most other countries, use today as their primary form of money is not physical cash created by the state, but the liabilities of banks. These liabilities were created through the accounting process that banks use when they make loans (Section 1.8). An efficient electronic payments system then ensures that these liabilities can function as money: most payments can be settled by electronically reducing the balance of one account and increasing the balance of another, without any physical transfer of cash. As we shall see in Chapter 2, this form of 'clearing' has been a function of banks as far back as historical records go. The vast majority of payments, by value, are made in this way.

We might object that the commercial banks are not really creating money – they are extending credit and this is not the same thing. The next chapter examines the nature and history of money in greater depth and concludes that in fact money is always best thought of as credit. But for now let us just consider whether it is really meaningful to describe the balance in your bank account as anything other than money. You can use it to pay for things, including your tax bill, and the government even guarantees that you will not lose it if the bank gets into trouble.*

While the idea that most new money is created by the likes of Barclays, HSBC, Lloyds, and the RBS rather than the Bank of England will be a surprise for most members of the public (although not as much of a shock as if you tried to convince them that their bank deposits were not really money at all), it is well known to those working in central banks. The following quotes testify to this and also confirm the point that bank deposits are, in essence, money:

> *In the United Kingdom, money is endogenous—the Bank supplies base money on demand at its prevailing interest rate, and broad money is created by the banking system.*
>
> Bank of England (1994)[13]

> *By far the largest role in creating broad money is played by the banking sector... When banks make loans they create additional deposits for those that have borrowed.*
>
> Bank of England (2007)[14]

---

* Balances up to £85,000 per person per banking group are guaranteed by the government under the Financial Services Compensation Scheme. Prior to October 2007 only the first £2,000 was fully covered, with 90 per cent of the next £33,000 covered. The guarantee was progressively raised during the financial crisis to try to maintain depositors' confidence and prevent any further bank runs after the run on Northern Rock.

Box 2: Building societies, credit unions and money creation

Building societies and credit unions also have the right to create money through issuing credit. Credit unions, however, have a range of strict controls on their credit creation power in the UK, more so than in many other countries.* At the time of writing this book, Credit Unions can only make loans to individuals, not to businesses or third sector organisations, and only to individuals living in a defined geographical area. In addition, they can only make loans up to £15,000. A Legislative Reform Order (LRO) is currently going through parliament to significantly liberalise these rules.[22] For the remainder of the book when we use the terms 'bank' or 'commercial/private bank' we also include building societies, which, like banks but unlike credit unions, have no legislative restrictions on their credit creation powers.

Money-creating organisations issue liabilities that are treated as media of exchange by others. The rest of the economy can be referred to as money holders.

Bank of England (2007)[15]

... changes in the money stock primarily reflect developments in bank lending as new deposits are created.

Bank of England (2007)[16]

Given the near identity of deposits and bank lending, Money and Credit are often used almost inseparably, even interchangeably...

Bank of England (2008)[17]

Each and every time a bank makes a loan, new bank credit is created – new deposits – brand new money.

Graham Towers (1939), former Governor of the central bank of Canada[18]

Over time... Banknotes and commercial bank money became fully interchangeable payment media that customers could use according to their needs.

European central bank (2000)[19]

The actual process of money creation takes place primarily in banks.

Federal Reserve Bank of Chicago (1961)[20]

In the Eurosystem, money is primarily created through the extension of bank credit... The commercial banks can create money themselves, the so-called giro money.

Bundesbank 2009[21]

---

* For a detailed discussion on the restrictions on credit unions credit creating power, see Werner, R. (2009). *Can credit unions create credit? An Analytical Evaluation of a Potential Obstacle to the Growth of Credit Unions.* Southampton: Centre for Banking, Finance and Sustainable Development, Discussion Paper Series, No. 2/09, p. 5.

There are two main ways of describing the process by which banks create money. The textbook model is given below, and we explain why we consider this model to be inaccurate. A more accurate model of the modern UK banking system, based on primary research, is described in Chapter 3.

1.6. Textbook descriptions: the multiplier model

Many undergraduates use a 'multiplier'* model of banking to explain how the 2.6 per cent of money that is cash is 'multiplied' up to create the 97.4 per cent that is simply liabilities of banks (i.e. numbers in bank accounts). The model is quite simple and runs as follows:

A member of the public deposits his salary of £1,000 into Bank A. The bank knows that, on average, the customer will not need the whole of his £1,000 returned at the same time – it is more likely that he will spend an average of £30 a day over the course of a month. Consequently, the bank assumes that much of the money deposited is 'idle' or spare and will not be needed on any particular day. It keeps (or is mandated to keep by the central bank) back a small 'reserve' of say 10 per cent of the money deposited with it (in this case £100), and lends out the other £900 to somebody who needs a loan.

Now both the original depositor and the new borrower think they have money (or more accurately, bank deposits) in their bank accounts – a total of £1,900 (£1,000 from the original deposit, plus £900 lent to the borrower).

This £900 is then spent in the economy, and the shop or business that receives that money deposits the money back into Bank B. Bank B then keeps £90 of this as its own reserve, while lending out the remaining £810. Again the process continues, with the £810 being spent and re-deposited in Bank C, who this time keeps a reserve of £81 while relending £729. At each point in the re-lending process, the sum balance of all the public's bank accounts increases, and in effect, new money, or purchasing power, has been created.

This process continues, with the amount being lent getting smaller at each stage, until after 204 cycles of this process the total amount of money, in the form of bank deposits (the total balance of the public's bank accounts) has grown to £10,000. Figure 2 shows this step-by-step process, with the additional lending (and the new money created as a result) shown in grey.

---

* For a classic account of the money multiplier, see Phillips (1920). *Bank Credit.* New York: Macmillan. For an explanation of how the system used to work in the United States, see: Nicols. (1992/1961). *Modern Money Mechanics: A workbook on Bank Reserves and Deposit Expansion.* Chicago: Federal Reserve Bank of Chicago. Retrieved from http://www.archive.org/stream/ModernMoneyMechanics/MMM#page/n1/mode/2up [accessed 29 April 2011].

Figure 2: The money multiplier model.

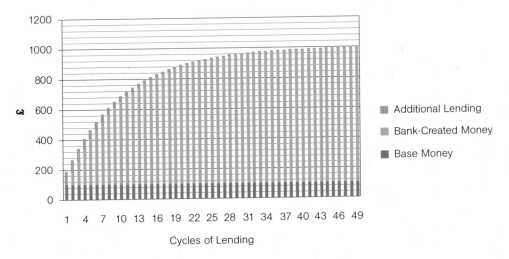

Cycles of Lending

This model implies three important things. First, it implies that banks cannot start lending without first having money deposited with them. In an economy with just a single bank, it would have to wait until someone deposited money in it before it could lend anything (the amount shown in dark green in Figure 2), whatever the reserve ratio. So this model supports the concept of banks being primarily intermediaries of money. The banks in this example can be thought of intermediating in succession, the outcome being 'credit creation' – the creation of new purchasing power in the bank accounts of the public.[23]

Secondly, this money multiplier model suggests that by altering the reserve ratio or the monetary base (cash plus central bank reserves), the central bank, Treasury, or government can closely control bank reserves and, through this, the amount of credit issued into the economy. If the reserve ratio is raised to 20 per cent by the government or central bank, for example, Bank A will only be able to lend out £80 instead of £90, Bank B £72 instead of £81, etc. Alternatively, if the amount of money at the base of the pyramid (Figure 3) is doubled, but the reserve ratio says at 10 per cent, then the total amount of money in the economy will also double.

Thirdly, it implies that the growth in the money supply of the economy is mathematically limited – as shown by the flattening of Figure 2. With a 10 per cent reserve ratio, there is an increase in the money supply for the first ~200 cycles, but after this point there is no discernable increase (because the amounts being effectively re-lent are infinitesimal). Even with a tiny reserve ratio of 2 per cent, the multiplier stops having an effect after around 1140 cycles (and in an

Figure 3: The money multiplier pyramid.

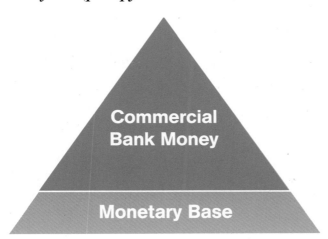

economy of 61 million people, the number of cycles of re-lending would take a few weeks at most).

This model of money creation can therefore be envisaged as a pyramid (Figure 3), where the central bank can control the total money supply by altering the size of the base (by controlling the amount of base money), and the steepness of the sides (by changing the reserve ratio).

Consequently, economists and policymakers following a simple textbook model of banking will assume that:

1. Banks are merely intermediaries and have no real control over the money supply of the economy.

2. Central banks can control the amount of money in the economy.

3. There is no possibility that growth in the money supply can get out of control because it is mathematically limited by the reserve ratio and the amount of base money.

Unfortunately this textbook model of banking is outdated and inaccurate and, as a result, these assumptions will be untrue.

1.7. Problems with the textbook model

The textbook model of banking implies that banks need depositors to start the money creation process. The reality, however, is that when a bank makes a loan it does not require anyone else's money to do so. Banks do not wait for deposits in order to make loans. Bank deposits are created by banks purely on the basis of their own confidence in the capacity of the borrower to repay the loan. As a Deputy Governor of the Bank England puts it:

> *Subject only but crucially to confidence in their soundness, banks extend credit by simply increasing the borrowing customer's current account, which can be paid away to wherever the borrower wants by the bank 'writing a cheque on itself'. That is, banks extend credit by creating money.*
>
> Paul Tucker, Deputy Governor at the Bank of England and member of the Monetary Policy Committee, 2007[24]

In the UK, there are currently no direct compulsory cash-reserve requirements placed on banks or building societies to restrict their lending (Section 5.3).* The main constraint on UK commercial banks and building societies is the need to hold enough liquidity reserves and cash to meet their everyday demand for payments.†

This means that the Bank of England cannot control bank money creation through adjusting the amount of central bank reserves that banks must hold, as in the multiplier model. In reality, rather than the Bank of England determining how much credit banks can issue, we could argue that it is the banks that determine how much central bank reserves and cash the Bank of England must lend to them. This will be explained in more detail in Chapter 3.

1.8. How money is actually created

Rather than the pyramid implied by the textbook model of money creation, the reality is closer to a 'balloon' of bank-created money wrapped around a core of base money (Figure 4).[25]

The Bank of England, given its own current choice of monetary policy instruments and tools, has relatively little direct control over the total amount of the balloon of commercial bank money, and therefore over the amount of money in the economy as a whole.

---

* The Financial Services Authority is currently bringing in legislation that will require Banks to hold an amount determined by 'stress testing' the potential for 100 per cent outflows of liabilities over a two-week period – see Financial Services Authority, October 2009, *PS09/16: Strengthening liquidity standards including feedback on CP08/22, CP09/13, CP09/14*. Retrieved from http://www.fsa.gov.uk/pages/Library/Policy/Policy/2009/09_16.shtml [accessed 14 May 2011]

† In the United States, for example, there is still a 10 per cent liquidity reserve ratio on certain deposits and in China the government actively changes its liquidity reserve ratio in an attempt to restrain credit creation in order to fight inflation – at the time of writing it stood at 20.5 per cent (having been raised for the fourth time in 2011. See *Financial Times* (17 April 2011). 'China raises bank reserve requirements'. The reserve requirement tool notwithstanding, the most important monetary policy tool in China remains its direct quota system for the quantity of credit creation, known as 'window guidance' (see Werner (2005) *op. cit.*).

Figure 4: 'Balloon' of commercial bank money.

This lack of control can be seen empirically over the last few decades. Prior to the crisis, the ratio between commercial bank money and base money increased so much that in 2006 there was £80 of commercial bank money for every £1 of base money.[26] This creation of money fuelled much of the unsustainable credit boom running up to 2007 (Figure 4).

Conversely, during the crisis the Bank of England's 'Quantitative Easing' scheme pumped £200 billion of new base money into the system (Figure 5), yet this had no noticeable impact on lending, since credit measure M4L continued to contract in 2010 and 2011. The only significant impact was a decrease in the ratio between commercial bank money and base money. This illustrates that banks' reserves with the central bank are not a very meaningful measure of money supply: they may indicate that the amount of money could potentially rise, but at any moment in time they do not measure money that is used for transactions or necessarily affecting the economy in any positive way. For instance, if the central bank creates more reserve money, as happened in Japan under the Bank of Japan's quantitative easing, then everything else being equal this does not in any way stimulate the economy. However, an increase in bank credit creation will have a positive impact on the value of economic transactions.

Figure 5: Collapse of commercial bank lending growth rate (M4L) and increase in central bank Reserves since Financial Crisis.

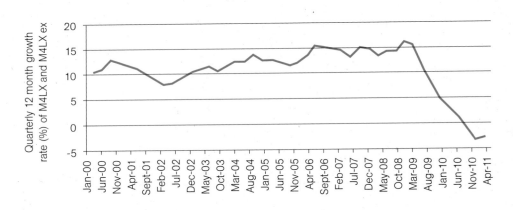

Growth rate of commercial bank lending
excluding securitisations (M4Lx) 2000-2011

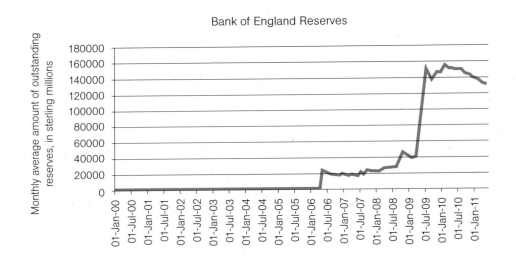

Bank of England Reserves

(Source: Bank of England)

Our research finds that the amount of money created by commercial banks is currently not actively determined by regulation, reserve ratios, or the control of the Bank of England, but largely by the confidence of the banks at any particular period in time. This is not to suggest that the Bank of England or the government could not intervene in order to influence or control money created by commercial banks. In other words, the authorities are not free of responsibility for results produced by the largely unchecked behaviour of the banking sector.

When banks are confident, they will create new money by creating credit and new bank deposits for borrowers. When they are fearful, they rein in lending, limiting the creation of new commercial bank money. The size of the commercial bank credit balloon, and therefore the money supply of the nation, depends mainly on the confidence and incentives of the banks. This pattern appears to be the case despite the Bank of England's implicit guaranteeing of the commercial banking system in terms of its 'Lender of Last Resort' function (promising to provide credit at times of crisis when no-one else will – see Section 2.5) and deposit insurance (see Section 3.6.1), policies that apply singularly to the banking sector.

The historical evidence, explored in Chapter 2, suggests that more important is the central bank's attitude to the regulation of credit itself. When a central bank chooses to adopt a laissez-faire policy concerning bank credit, as now in the UK, boom-bust credit cycles are likely to result, with all their implications for economic analysis and policy. This is in contrast to an earlier period, where, as we show in Chapter 2, the Bank of England, like most central banks, imposed credit growth quotas on banks; such credit controls were abolished in the early 1970s (Section 2.6.3).

If you are keen to understand in more depth exactly how money is created by the banking system today, then you may wish to skip ahead to Chapter 3. However, it is important to see how money and banking have developed over time to give us the current system. In the next chapter we shall see that political and economic developments, coupled with financial innovations, led to a situation where bank-created credit-money (henceforth 'commercial bank money') came to be accepted by the state and eventually came to dominate the monetary system.

2. THE NATURE AND HISTORY OF MONEY AND BANKING

*The significance of money as expressing the relative value of commodities is
… quite independent of any intrinsic value. Just as it is irrelevant whether a
[physical measuring instrument] consists of iron, wood or glass, since only the
relation of its parts to each other or to another measure concerns us, so the scale
that money provides for the determination of values has nothing to do with the
nature of its substance. This ideal significance of money as a standard and an
expression of the value of goods has remained completely unchanged, whereas its
character as an intermediary, as a means to store and to transport values, has
changed in some degree and is still in the process of changing.*

Georg Simmel (1907), Sociologist and Philosopher[27]

*Money is not metal. It is trust inscribed. And it does not seem to matter much
where it is inscribed: on silver, on clay, on paper, on a liquid crystal display.*

Niall Ferguson (2009), Historian[28]

2.1. The functions of money

Money is clearly fundamental to capitalist systems. It is hard to envisage a
modern economy without it. While the medium of money may change with
technological developments – from coins to notes to cheques to credit and
debit cards and online e-payments – the activity of exchanging, storing, and
accumulating units of value called money has been with us for centuries and
shows no sign of going away.

Yet money and banking, as subjects for serious examination in their own right,
have been largely neglected by orthodox economics over the past 60–70 years.
This seems strange, since, with the exception of a brief period of stability from
the end of WWII to 1970, we have seen an increase in the frequency and
severity of both currency and banking crises, culminating in the global financial
crisis of 2008/2009, the most severe since the Great Depression of the 1930s.[*]

---

[*] Prior to 2003, there have been 96 currency crises since 1970, the year before the US dollar was de-coupled from Gold. Kaminsky, G. L. (2003). *Varieties of Currency Crises, National Bureau of Economic Research*, Working Paper 10193. Retrieved from http://www.nber.org/papers/w10193

Let us start with trying to understand what money is for. Money is generally described by economists in terms of its functions rather than any kind of overarching property or essence. It is generally viewed as having four key functions:[29]

1. **Store of value** – holding on to money gives us confidence in our future ability to access goods and services – it gives us future 'purchasing power'.

2. **Medium of exchange** – enables us to conduct efficient transactions and trade with each other. Money enables us to move beyond barter relations which require both parties to have exactly the right quality and quantity of a commodity to make an exchange – a 'double coincidence of wants'.[30]

3. **Unit of account** – without a widely agreed upon unit of measurement we cannot settle debts or establish effective price systems, both key elements of capitalist economies.

Related to item 3, a means of final payment or **settlement**.

Whilst there is some consensus that these four functions are all important in constituting money, there is less agreement about their relative importance and their role in the origins of money and relationship to banking. We explore two major theories of money* to elaborate this issue as it lies at the heart of our challenge of understanding money and banking properly.

2.2. Commodity theory of money: money as natural and neutral

2.2.1. Classical economics and money

Classical economists, Adam Smith, John Stuart Mill, David Ricardo, and Karl Marx, argued that real economic value lay not in money but in land, labour, and the process of trade and exchange. Money is simply a symbol representing that value. Mill, for example, stated that money's existence 'does not interfere with the operation of any laws of value' and that:

> *There cannot, in short, be intrinsically a more insignificant thing, in the economy of society, than money; except in the character of a contrivance for sparing time and labour. It is a machine for doing quickly and commodiously*

---

* There are many other theories and 'schools' of money than the two described here, not least Austrian, Post-Keynesian, 'Circuitist', Marxist, Feminist and Green but these are the two that have come to greatest prominence in the academic literature. Goodhart, C.A.E. (1998). The two concepts of money: implications for the analysis of optimal currency areas. *European Journal of Political Economy* 14: 407–432. Smithin, J. (2000). Introduction in *What is Money?* London and New York, Routledge, pp.1–16. Useful guides to different schools of thought on money include Smithin, J. (2000). *op. cit.* and Ingham, G. (ed). (2005).*Concepts of Money: Interdisciplinary Perspectives from Economics, Sociology and Political Science.* London: Edward Elgar.

what would be done, though less quickly and commodiously, without it; and, like many other kinds of machinery, it only exerts a distinct and independent influence of its own when it gets out of order.[31]

The classical economics account of money is as a way of optimising the efficiency of exchange. It 'naturally' emerges from barter relations as people find certain commodities to be widely acceptable and begin to use them as media of exchange rather than keeping or consuming them.[32]

Commodities with the three, most money-like properties (intrinsic value, portability, divisibility, homogeneity) naturally become adopted as money over time. Hence, gold and silver coins, possessing all three properties, became the dominant medium for money, according to the classical account.[33] In the orthodox story, where optimal money-like commodities are not available, alternatives will naturally appear. The classic example is the prisoner-of-war camp where cigarettes became a substitute for money.[34] Cigarettes were widely available (prisoners were usually given an equal amount along with other rations), fairly homogenous, reasonably durable, and of a convenient size for the smallest or, in packets, for the largest transactions (divisible). The centrality of the commodity itself in determining the nature of money led to this theory being called the 'commodity theory of money' or the 'metallist theory of money'.

As the economist Joseph Schumpeter describes it, the logic of this argument leads to a conception of money as a neutral, imaginary 'veil' lying over the 'real' economy:[35]

> *'Real analysis' proceeds from the principle that all essential phenomena of economic life are capable of being described in terms of goods and services, of decisions about them and of relations between them. Money enters the picture only in the modest role of a technical device that has been adopted in order to facilitate transactions... so long as it functions normally, it does not affect the economic process, which behaves in the same way as it would in a barter economy: this is essentially what the concept of Neutral Money implies.*

2.2.2. Neoclassical economics and money

Modern neoclassical economics built on this conception of neutral exchange-optimising money as it developed 'scientific' models of the economy in the late nineteenth and twentieth century based on mathematical rules of supply and demand.[36] In these 'general equilibrium' models, which still dominate the economics profession today, 'real' transactions – those involving goods and services – are facilitated by the existence of money but money itself has no significant role.

Under the conditions of 'perfect information' that are assumed for markets to 'clear', (where the quantity supplied meets the quantity demanded) people 'automatically' exchange goods and services, without delay or friction, according to the production costs of the commodity and people's 'marginal utility' – that is, the balance between the convenience obtained and the risk avoided from its possession.[37]

This approach posed a question for how to include money. French economist Leon Walras created a hypothetical numeraire (a symbolic representation of existing commodity values) to enable him to model an exchange economy in which the market 'clears' under conditions of equilibrium. To do so, Walras had to postulate the existence of an omnipotent 'auctioneer' capable of knowing all exchange and utility values at all times. This deity enabled Walras to happily ignore money.

But other economists were not happy with the 'imaginary auctioneer'. Since money was a commodity, it must also have a production function and, since everyone wants it, also a utility function. What was special about money was that it had unique properties of durability and very high velocity (speed at which it circulates through the economy in transactions), both of which reduced its relative production costs to near zero.[38] Hence, in orthodox economic theory, the demand for money can be understood almost entirely through its marginal utility.[39] And this was presumed to be relatively constant, in the long run at least, since money was simply representative of the value of other 'real' commodities.* Hence money was built in to models of general equilibrium with the concept of its neutrality effectively maintained. Mainstream macroeconomic models today treat money this way, by including a 'money-in-utility' function that attempts to show why people desire money, whilst preserving its neutrality.[40]

2.2.3. *Problems with the orthodox story*

If this description of the role of money in the economy seems a little strange to you, you will be pleased to know you are not alone in questioning it. Any economic model requires generalisations, assumptions, and simplifications in order to tell us something interesting about how things work. But in the case of orthodox economics description of the relationship between human beings and money, the assumptions are so far-fetched that they fatally undermine the model.

---

* Fisher, I. (1911). *The Purchasing Power of Money*. New York: Macmillan. Fisher formulated this approach with the equation of exchange which states that under any given conditions of industry and civilization, deposits tend to hold a fixed or normal ratio to money in circulation. The equation of exchange is $MV = PT$, where M is Money (including bank deposits), V is the velocity of money, P is the general price level and T, the volume of transactions.

The most obvious failure is that the theory is internally inconsistent. If you take the assumption of perfect information to its logical conclusion, there would be no need for money or indeed any other kind of intermediating financial service (including banking) in the economy at all.* For if everyone did indeed have perfect information at all times about everything, as with Walras's auctioneer, they really would exchange goods and services in barter-like fashion without the need for any commodity like money to provide them with information about the value of those goods and services. So, paradoxically, under conditions of perfect information and certainty, money becomes redundant, which of course undermines neoclassical explanations of the origins of money in commodity-exchange in the first place.† This circularity has been grappled with by proponents of general equilibrium models ever since.[41]

But it is not necessary to conduct these kinds of thought experiments to realise the logical inconsistency of the orthodox story. Think about any of the successful entrepreneurs you know. You will probably find that most of them started out with very little money and had to get loans from the bank, friends, or family before they could begin selling their services or products on the market. As Marx pointed out, in the capitalist system, money (or capital/financing) is required prior to production,[42] rather than naturally arising after production as a way of making exchange more convenient. This is why it is called 'capital-ism'. So building a model that starts with market clearing and allocation and then tries to fit in money as a veil on top of this makes little sense. As American economist Hyman Minsky argues:

> *... we cannot understand how our economy works by first solving allocation problems and then adding financing relations; in a capitalist economy resource allocation and price determination are integrated with the financing of outputs, positions in capital assets, and the validating of liabilities. This means that nominal values (money prices) matter: money is not neutral.*[43]

Besides this, there is no explanation of how money is injected into the economy in the first place and in what quantity. Money is simply called forth by individual demand – but there is no account for how and why individuals

---

* For a comprehensive and amusing list of the activities and organisations that would not exist under conditions of perfect information see Werner, R. (2005) *op. cit.*, pp. 20–24; they include insurance, advertising, consultancy, legal advice, estate agents, economic forecasting, meetings, stockbroking, fund management and securitization.

† The historical evidence of 'pure barter' economies is also lacking. Anthropologists argue that there has never been such a thing as a 'pure bartering economy' as hypothesized by classical economists, and hence call into question the emergence of money from barter – see Mauss, M. (1966). *The Gift*, London: Cohen & West.
Humphrey maintains that 'The search for coincidence of wants is not necessary, since the time and place of barter for common items was established long in the past' and that barter 'has been misconstrued largely because of the persistence of the creation-myth in classical and neoclassical economics that in barter lie the origins of money and hence of modern capitalism.' Humphrey, C., (1985) "Barter and Economic Disintegration" *Man*, 20 (March): 48-72, p56).

handle money or why the demand for or supply of money is at a certain level at a particular point of time.[44]

In addition, the notion that money might be used as a store of value and hence not immediately put back into circulation cannot be easily incorporated into general equilibrium models as the velocity of money is assumed to be stable in the long run. Keynes, writing during the 1930s at the time of the Great Depression, argued that the demand for money was much more complex than the orthodox story allows: in a 'monetary economy' (as opposed to a 'real' economy) people choose to hoard (save) money under certain conditions as well as using it as a means of exchange.[45]

Neither does the orthodox story provide a satisfactory explanation of the existence of modern 'fiat' money – that is, money backed only by the authority of a sovereign (previously the King, now the state or central bank) rather than any commodity. The £10 banknote in your wallet or the £400 of digital money deposited in your bank account does not appear to be backed by any commodity. You cannot change it into gold or silver.

2.3. Credit theory of money: money as a social relationship

Have a look in your wallet to see if you have any sterling notes. Notice that on a £10 note it states that 'I promise to pay the bearer on demand the sum of ten pounds'. It appears this money is a future claim upon others – a social relationship of credit and debt between two agents. This relationship is between the issuer of the note, in this case the state, and the individual. It does not appear to have anything to do with relations of production (between an agent and an object) or the exchange of commodities (object-object relations).

The orthodox economics narrative rests upon deductive* assumptions about reality that enable the construction of abstract models.[46] In contrast, researchers who have chosen a more inductive approach, investigating empirically how money and banking actually works, have been more likely to favour the view that money is fundamentally a social relation of credit and debt. These researchers of money come from various academic disciplines. They include heterodox economists (including some early twentieth-century economists), anthropologists, monetary and financial historians, economic sociologists and geographers, and political economists.[47,48,49,50,51,52] In fact, they only thing

---

* Deductive reasoning is concerned with whether conclusions logically follow from a set of assumptions. We can have an argument that is sound, but its usefulness is questionable if the assumptions do not fit well with our experience of the real world. This approach contrasts with inductive reasoning which attempts to draw conclusions from empirical observations. These conclusions are more grounded in evidence, but provide less certainty in the argument because they are always vulnerable to being refuted by new observations that contradict our previous experience.

they have in common in terms of their academic discipline is that they are not neoclassical economists.

2.3.1. *Money as credit: historical evidence*

From a historical perspective, the earliest detailed written evidence of monetary relations is to be found in the financial system of Babylon and ancient Egypt. These civilisations used banking systems thousands of years before the first evidence of commodity money (coinage).[53] As today, the banks consisted of accounting-entry payment systems (i.e. lists or tallies of credits and debts). As the monetary historian Glynn Davies puts it:

> *Literally hundreds of thousands of cuneiform blocks have been unearthed by archaeologists in the various city sites along the Tigris and Euphrates, many of which were deposit receipts and monetary contracts, confirming the existence of simple banking operations as everyday affairs, common and widespread throughout Babylonia. The code of Hammurabi, law-giver of Babylon, who ruled from about 1792 to 1750 BC, gives us categorical evidence, available for our inspection in the shape of inscriptions on a block of solid diorite standing over 7ft high now in the Paris Louvre, showing that by this period 'Bank Operations by temples and great landowners had become so numerous and so important' that it was thought 'necessary to lay down standard rules of procedure'.[54]*

The historical record suggests that banking preceded coined money by thousands of years. Indeed, historical evidence points to the written word having its origins in the keeping of accounts. The earliest Sumerian numerical accounts consisted of a stroke for units and simple circular depression for tens.[55]

These banks conducted 'clearing' or 'bookkeeping' activities (also often described as 'giro-banking' – giro from the Greek 'circle'). If enough people recorded their debts with a single bank, that bank would be in a position to cancel out different debts through making adjustments to different accounts without requiring the individuals to be present. Modern banks still undertake this clearing activity by entering numbers into computers as we shall see in Chapter 3.

Whilst clay tablets were used in Babylon, tally sticks were used in Europe for many centuries to record debts.[56] Tally sticks were sticks of hazel-wood, notched to indicate the amount of the purchase or debt, created when the buyer became a debtor by accepting a good or services from the seller who automatically became the creditor. They were used in England until 1826 and can still be seen in the British Museum today.[57]

Another historical argument is that the practice of measuring value came from elaborate compensation schedules – Wergeld – developed to prevent blood feuds in primitive societies.[58,59] These required measuring the debt one owed for injuries, actual and imagined, inflicted on others. These became increasingly formalised and determined in public assemblies as societies developed. In contrast to the orthodox story, they were not the result of individual negotiation or exchange.[60] The nature and value of these items was determined by the relative severity of the injury and the ease of access to the item (they would be commonly available) and had nothing to do with their exchange or use value. 'Geld' or 'Jeld' was the Old English and Old Frisian term for money, and is still used in Dutch and German.[61]

Both these examples of tallies and compensation show money as tokens, not necessarily having any intrinsic value, which record a social relationship between credit and debtor.

2.3.2. *The role of the state in defining money*

Another important part of the story has been the role of the state in ensuring the acceptability of such tokens. Standardisation occurred with the development of upper classes and temple, and later palaces and communities. Evidence points to the common origins of money, debts, and writing in the tax levies of the palaces.[62]

One strand of monetary theory, known as Chartalism, argues that as palaces expanded their domains, tax payments became standardised in terms of quantities or weights of widely used commodities, such as wheat or barley. These formed the basis for all the early 'money of account' units, such as the mina, shekel, lira, and pound. Money originated then, not as a cost-minimising medium of exchange as in the orthodox story, but as the unit of account in which debts to the palace, specifically tax liabilities, were measured.[63,64]

It is the state's coercive power to tax its citizens that defines the unit of account as the primary function of money, as Mitchell Innes stated in 1913:

> *The government by law obliges certain selected persons to become its debtors. This procedure is called levying a tax, and the persons thus forced into this position of debtors to the government must in theory seek out the holders of the tallies and acquire from them the tallies by selling to them some commodity in exchange for which they may be induced to part with their tallies. When these are returned to the government treasury, the taxes are paid.[65]*

Financier and heterodox economist Warren Mosler uses the metaphor of a household currency to try to make clear the relationship between the state and citizens:

> *The story begins with parents creating coupons they then use to pay their children for doing various household chores. Additionally, to 'drive the model,' the parents require the children to pay them a tax of 10 coupons a week to avoid punishment. This closely replicates taxation in the real economy, where we have to pay our taxes or face penalties. The coupons are now the new household currency. Think of the parents as 'spending' these coupons to purchase 'services' (chores) from their children. With this new household currency, the parents, like the federal government, are now the issuer of their own currency.*[66]

The state then defines the unit of account as that which it 'accepts at public pay offices, mainly in payment of taxes'.[67] The government's acceptance underpins the broader acceptability of these tokens. However, Febrero[68] and others have criticised the Chartalist school of thought for overstating the extent to which money and credit creation is a creature of the state rather than the private sector.* The usefulness of bank deposits lies just as much in the ability to use them to repay liabilities to others as to the state.

As we have seen, the means of payment varied over time, but for many centuries the instrument used was not coins. When coins did come into common usage, rarely was the nominal value of coins the same as the value of the metal of which they were made.[69] Instead, the state determined the value of the coin and was free to change it whenever it felt like it.† In England, Queen Elizabeth I established in 1560/1561 a setting of four ounces of sterling silver as the invariant standard for the pound unit of account. Incredibly, this setting lasted until World War I, the longest historically recorded period for an unchanging unit of account in any state.[70]

---

* A further criticism of Chartalism is that the theory does not take sufficient account of the differences between the US and EU systems. Under the Maastricht Treaty, the EU prevents central banks from directly funding government debt, which is one reason why under quantitative easing the Bank of England purchased gilts through the secondary markets rather than directly from the government.

† The state has, historically, used violent coercion to enforce the use of and taxation in national currencies, including execution, imprisonment and branding with the coin. In nineteenth-century colonial Africa, for example, taxation backed by severe punishment for non-payment was used to coerce subjugated populations into wage labour and tax would be pitched at a level that elicited the required amount of work (Wray [1998] *op. cit.* pp. 57–61). On the link between money and violence see also: Tolstoy, L. (1904). What shall we do then? On the Moscow Census Collected Articles. London: J.M. Dent & Co. Central banks also have a long record of banning or taxing out of existence private or local currency systems, not least the 5000 currencies that were estimated to circulate in the United States at the beginning of the twentieth century. See Zelizer, V. (1997 [1994]). *The Social Meaning of Money: Pin Money, Paychecks, Poor Relief, and Other Currencies.* Princeton, New Jersey: Princeton University Press, p. 17).

However, the use of metal coins through the ages does not unsettle the central conception of money as being created through credit/debt relationships rather than depending on, or even deriving from, the intrinsic value of an underlying commodity to give it its 'money-ness'.* As historian Niall Ferguson says, 'Money is not metal. It is trust inscribed.'[71] The long period of the use of gold and silver coins as the tokens of choice to represent money may be one explanation for the powerful grip that the commodity theory of money has on the imagination. Another may be the history of the development of modern banking, and the role of the goldsmiths of London in the story.

2.4. Key historical developments: promissory notes, fractional reserves and bonds

The origins of modern banking in Europe and the UK are a complex mixture of constitutional, fiscal, and monetary developments and there is not room for an in-depth historical account in this book.[†] Instead, we will review briefly three key financial innovations that have given rise to the modern monetary system:

1. The emergence of private media of exchange (Bills of Exchange) in the form of **promissory notes** that circulated independently of state money, which at the time was mainly gold and silver coinage.

2. The practice, by the custodians and exchangers of precious metals and coinage, of issuing deposit receipts to a value greater than the value of deposits the custodians actually possessed – a practice that would later be described as **fractional reserve banking**.

3. The perceived need for a stable source of long-term borrowing by governments from the custodians and exchangers of precious metals – a practice that would come to be known as **bond issuance**.

All three of these innovations came fatefully together in Britain in the seventeenth century, a time of almost continual warfare.[‡] At the time, silver coinage was the state currency. Crown and Parliament were in a constant struggle to raise enough taxes and mint enough silver coinage to meet the resulting debts.[72]

---

* Whether it might be *sensible* or *desirable* to pin the value of money to a commodity such as gold is a different question entirely

† See Ingham (2004) *op. cit.* pp.107–133 for a guide to developments at a European level and Davies (2004) *op. cit.* pp. 238–283 for a British focus. See Werner (2005) *op. cit.* Chapter 12, for an overview of the history of banking and its implications.

‡ These included the Civil War (1642–1652) and colonial wars with Spain, Holland and France. Retrieved from http://en.wikipedia.org/wiki/List_of_wars_involving_England#17th_century [accessed 17 April 2011].

This also meant that there was not much demand for luxury goods at the time, including jewellery. As their name suggests, goldsmiths' original task was fashioning jewellery from precious metals. But goldsmiths also played a useful custodial and exchange role – their vaults were secure places to keep gold and silver coin, bullion, and jewels. And as London grew in prominence, attracting traders from across Europe, the goldsmiths, along with other professions such as pawnbrokers and scriveners (someone who could read and write), became important holders and exchangers of domestic and foreign coinage.[73] The 'seizure of the mint' by King Charles I in 1640 coupled with the outbreak of civil war 1642 led to a significant increase in demand for their custodial services in particular.[74]

2.4.1. Promissory notes

Goldsmiths would issue 'deposit receipts' to people who left gold and silver coins with them. These were simple acknowledgements of a personalised debt relationship between the goldsmith and the owner of the gold placed in their care; the earliest known such receipt, issued to Laurence Hoare, dates back to 1633.[75] Goldsmiths also began to carry out clearing and bookkeeping activities.[*] Everyone soon found that it was a lot easier simply to use the deposit receipts directly as a means of payment. The bankers' deposit receipts effectively became a medium of exchange, much as had the Bills of Exchange that began circulating through Europe considerably earlier.[†]

2.4.2. Fractional reserve banking

Goldsmiths also soon realised that they could lend out a proportion of the metallic coins they kept safe since it was inconceivable that all of their customers would choose to withdraw all of their deposits at exactly the same time. By charging interest on these loans (the rules on usury had been considerably liberalised in England to a 5 per cent interest rate maximum), goldsmiths were able to make a good and exponentially growing return on this service for very little effort.[76]

---

[*] The first regular banker was reputed to be Mr Francis Child, a goldsmith who kept a shop on Fleet Street, London, who was followed in the practice by Messrs Snow and Dunne on the same street. See Percy, R. (1824) *Interesting memorials of its rise, progress, & present state, Volume 3* (Google eBook). Child & Co is still operating as a private bank today and is owned by the Royal Bank of Scotland.

[†] In sixteenth century Latin Christian Europe, Central Europe and Italy in particular, early forms of privately issued credit money called 'Bills of exchange' or 'Bills of Trade' came in to being. Networks of traders, integrated through regular interactions on established trade routes and cities, began to accept these Bills in lieu of payment in the coinage of the period, determined by city-states of the time. In the German lands, these Bills were traded and settled in regular intervals at the major trade fairs (Messe).If one merchant owed another a sum of money which could not be paid in cash until the conclusion of a transaction some months hence, the creditor could draw a bill on the debtor and either use the bill as a means of payment its own right or obtain cash for it at a discount from a banker willing to act as a broker. Ferguson. (2008). op. cit. pp. 43–44.

Soon goldsmiths further realised that as the real deposit receipts were being used as a means of exchange (as opposed to the metal) they could equally issue deposit receipts instead of actual metal for their loans. And this meant they could issue more gold deposit receipts than they had actual gold deposited with them. Goldsmiths chose to keep just a fraction of their total loan value in the form of gold in their vaults.* Thus they created new money and **fractional reserve banking** was born. In the words of financial journalist Hartley Withers:

> ... *some ingenious goldsmith conceived of the epoch making notion of giving notes not only to those who had deposited metal, but also to those who came to borrow it, and so founded banking.*[77]

As has been pointed out by a range of different scholars, from a legal perspective, the goldsmiths were committing fraud.[78] Their deposit receipts, when issued to those borrowing (as opposed to depositing) gold from them, stated that the goldsmith actually held in reserve the gold that they were borrowing. This was simply not true – no deposit had been made and the gold was not there. The receipts were fictitious – they were pure credit and had nothing to do with gold. But no-one could tell the difference between a real deposit receipt and a fictitious one. As Karl Marx describes the process in Das Kapital:

> *With the development of interest-bearing capital and the credit system, all capital seems to double itself, and sometimes treble itself, by the various modes in which the same capital, or perhaps even the same claim on a debt, appears in different forms in different hands. The greater portion of this 'money-capital' is purely fictitious. All the deposits, with the exception of the reserve fund, are merely claims on the banker, which, however, never exist as deposits.*[79]

Aside from its questionable legality, fractional reserve banking was and remains a business model quite different from normal market-based activities.[80] For most businesses, there is a direct relationship between revenues and the provision of goods and services and hence costs, usually at a declining rate. And in true intermediary banking activity, for example, the loaning of time deposits as described at the start of this chapter, profits are limited by the interest-rate differential between what the bank has to pay to the saver and demand from the borrower.

---

* Accounts of fractional reserve type activities outside the UK go back much earlier than the goldsmiths however. For a thorough ranging review see Huerta de Soto, J. (2006/1998). *Money, Bank Credit, and Economic Cycles*, translated from the Spanish by Stroup, M.A., Alabama: Ludvig von Mises Institute., Chapter 2, pp 37–111; For a user-friendly and colourful introduction to the origins of fractional reserve banking, download Paul Grignon's animated film *Money as Debt*. Retrieved from http://video.google.com/videoplay?docid=-2550156453790090544#

Box 3: Bonds, securities, and gilts

A **bond** is a debt instrument which enables companies or states to access cash through issuing an IOU to an investor. The investor, who could be an individual but these days is more often an institutional investor (e.g. a pension fund) loans a certain amount of money, for a certain amount of time, with a certain interest rate, to the company or country. In return, the investor receives a certificate which they can use to redeem the bond when it matures (i.e. the date at which it expires). Meanwhile, a fixed payment is usually made by the issuer to the holder (the coupon). This is why bonds are also called **fixed income securities**. Furthermore, when market interest rates rise, the value of bonds falls, and vice versa, as the value of the expected future income stream from the fixed coupon payment changes. Bonds are an example of **debt based securities** or **tradeable securities** (**stocks** are **equity based securities**).

Bonds issued by companies are generally termed **commercial bonds**, **commercial paper** (which are for a shorter term than bonds) or **commercial securities**.

Bonds issued by states have a variety of names, including **government bonds**, **government securities, Treasury bills** (which refer to short-term government bonds) and in the UK they are referred to as **gilts**. The term gilt or **gilt-edged security** originated from the gilded edges of the certificates themselves, and has come to represent the primary characteristic of gilts as an investment: that they have proved safe investments over time. The British government has never (yet) failed to make interest or principal payments on gilts as they fall due.

Bonds can be issued by a government in foreign currencies; these are often referred to as **sovereign bonds**.

Because most governments do not default, government bonds are an attractive form of investment, in particular for risk-averse investors such as pension funds. For the same reason, government bonds can be highly 'liquid' or 'tradeable'. So-called **benchmark bonds**, with high issuance volumes, can often be sold very rapidly in exchange for cash or bank money, which are the final means of payment in modern societies.

But by lending at interest through fractional reserve banking, the revenue stream can rise exponentially, without the provision of any new goods or services to anyone, and hence without further costs (see also Box 8, Section 3.4). A bank can charge compound interest, for example, on its loan, whereby interest incurred is added to the principal loan and further interest charged upon both the principal and the additional interest on an ongoing basis.[81] The bank has not paid any equivalent interest to any saver in order to create the loan – it has simply created a highly profitable stream of income backed by nothing more than the perceived ability of the borrower to repay the loan or the collateral owned by the borrower (in this case their home).* This is not to say that the bank has not provided a valuable service to the borrower by extending credit, and so therefore some profit is justified by the increased liquidity risk that the bank runs as a result of the additional credit – although such liquidity risk may in the end be directly or indirectly underwritten by the community).

2.4.3. *Bond issuance and the creation of the Bank of England*

With their ability to create new credit seemingly from nowhere, it was not surprising that goldsmiths were popular. Soon the King and Parliament, unable to raise enough taxes or mint silver coinage quickly enough to meet the demands of the Civil War and French wars of the period, began to borrow from goldsmiths, too. The demand for goldsmiths' lending services, from both private individuals and government grew to be so profitable that in order to boost their deposits they began to offer to pay interest on 'time deposits' – that is, deposits left for a guaranteed period of time. Any remaining doubts about the negotiability and status of goldsmiths' notes was removed in the Promissory Notes Act of 1704 which confirmed the legality of the common practices that goldsmiths had being employing since the 1640s.[82]

The state's informal and eventually legal acceptance of goldsmiths' fictitious deposit receipts increased the state's spending power and allowed the creation of modern commercial bank money. Commercial bank money was already in use in seventeenth-century Holland and Sweden; it was now developed in England. These countries were engaged in wars at the time and were short of money. As a result, they took to issuing bonds (Box 3) to the rich merchants and goldsmiths of their respective countries. The practice of bond issuance had begun much earlier in the city states of northern Italy and was another transformative financial innovation – a way for the state and later companies to fund expansionary trade through long-term borrowing without the need for additional metal coinage.[83]

The Dutch brought the concept to England following the successful invasion by the Dutch Prince William III of Orange in the Glorious Revolution of 1688. After repeated defaults by indebted kings and a raid on the national mint, Parliament and creditors of the state (the merchants and goldsmiths of London) lobbied for the creation of a privately owned Bank with public

---

* There is some confusion in the various debates around the role of interest and fractional reserve banking literature about which is more important. We would argue that there is not a problem with non-compounding interest when it genuinely represents the lost opportunity cost of not having a resource (in this case money). But in the case of fractional reserve banking, as we have seen, there is no loss of resource by the bank when it makes a loan – no money is being taken from anywhere else. For a useful guide to the historical use of interest see Pettifor, A. (2006) *The Coming First World Debt Crisis,* Basingstoke: Palgrave Macmillan, Chapter 5, pp. 120–144.

privileges – the Bank of England – and the secession of one square mile of central London as a quasi-sovereign state within the state.* The merchants loaned £1.2 million to the state at 8 per cent interest, which was funded by hypothecated customs and excise revenues.[84] The English state had begun to issue bonds and borrow at interest. For the first time, the state committed a proportion of its tax revenues towards the interest payments on long term debts.[85] This system of private credit creation superseded the former system of public money issuance in the form of tallies issued by the Treasury. To symbolise this, tally sticks were buried in the Bank of England's foundations. This was the first time taxation became a tool for the state to repay debts to wealthy private sector creditors.

The Bank of England was created in 1694 and three years later was granted a royal charter and the right to take deposits, issue bank notes, and discount promissory notes. The promissory notes that had previously circulated only amongst the goldsmiths and trader networks, could now be traded at the Bank of England (at a discounted rate) for the state money.

The two major monetary innovations of the period – public debt in the form of state bond issuance and promissory notes – were now integrated for the first time in history in a single institution: the newly created, privately owned Bank of England. In this new arrangement, the state now raised taxes at least partially to fund interest payments on its debts to the creditor class. And at the same time, the previously private deposit receipts now became accepted, at a discounted rate, by Bank of England.[†] They were now just one small step from being equivalent to state-money, which at the time was coinage, which could be accepted as tax.

2.5. Early monetary policy: the Bullionist debates and 1844 Act

The new integration of the state and its creditor class proved to be successful for England and is often held up as one of the key reasons for its defeat of France in the war that followed and for the expansion of English commercial, trade, and military power.[86,87] It was a model that was eventually imitated over much of the rest of the Western world. Yet, the Bank was less successful at preventing

---

* The City of London Corporation, the municipal authority for London's financial district, has unusual powers to this day, often expressed in ceremonial oddities such the granting of 'permission' from the Lord Mayor for the Queen to cross the City boundaries, as well as unique features of more practical importance such as the ability of corporations and partnerships to vote in elections, its own police, and the power to amend its own constitution. For fascinating detail about the 'offshore tax haven' in the middle of London, see Chapter 12 of Shaxson, N. (2010). *Treasure Islands: Tax Havens and the Men Who Stole the World*. London: Random House.

† As Carruthers (1996) *op. cit.*, p. 130, notes, shortly after the establishment of the Bank of England, the Promissory Notes Act of 1704 made all notes, whether payable to 'X', to 'X or order', or to 'X or bearer', legally transferable, giving credit money a public monetary sphere.

volatility in the issuance of paper money and coinage. Whilst, in London, private banks were gradually absorbed into the Bank of England, elsewhere in the UK industrialists were forming regional commercial banks – or 'country banks' – which played an important role in the industrial revolution.[88] These did not have access to the backing of the central bank as lender of last resort and relied on working through accounts at London clearing banks. The country banks issued paper notes of various types and qualities which were discounted (i.e. exchanged for Bank of England notes or credit entries in banks' accounts with the Bank of England) at relatively low rates of interest.[89]

Despite the Bank of England's notes being linked to gold, currency and banking crises remained frequent and inflation rampant. A great debate began between two schools of thought over how best to solve the problem, a debate which continues to this day in modern monetary theory.* The Bullionist (later 'Currency') school claimed that rising prices were the fault of the Bank of England for discounting too great a volume of bills issued by private banks. Convinced of the intrinsic value and stability of gold (the commodity theory money – Section 2.2), they called for the return of full convertibility of bank-note issuance to gold reserves. In contrast, the anti-Bullionist (later 'Banking') school claimed that rising prices were a natural result of increased economic activity and trade, resulting in a natural increase in the price of gold and the demand for loans.[90]

As financial crises continued into the first half of the nineteenth century, the government eventually acted. First, the Bank Charter Act 1833 made Bank of England notes legal tender for the first time in England and Wales. In addition, the act abandoned the 5 per cent usury laws for the Bank of England's discounting facility. The hope was that by increasing the discount rate, the Bank could suppress the issuance of notes by private banks by driving up the cost of converting them into legal tender. As Davies suggests, 'in this quiet way, what was to become the famed 'Bank Rate' instrument of policy for the next 150 years was born'.[91]

But these measures proved not to be sufficient to create financial stability. Further banking failures in 1836 and 1839 led to massive drains on the Bank of England's gold reserves as customers feared that their privately issued bank-notes would become inconvertible. Finally, the 1844 Bank Charter Act banned the creation of any new banks with note-issuing powers (including

---

* See Galbraith (1975) *op. cit.* pp. 48–49, for a brief review of the debate. The Banking versus Currency school debate was later continued in the main dividing line in twentieth-century monetary theory between the Monetarist school who believed the government could determine the money supply exogenously through changing the base rate and the neo- or post-Keynesian school which viewed credit creation as 'endogenously' determined by the economy itself.

amalgamations of existing banks) and limited the issue of new notes by the Bank of England.[92] What English economist and journalist Walter Bagehot described as the 'cast iron' system limited the issue of new notes to the existing £14 million in circulation that were backed by government securities.[93] Beyond that, any new notes issued would have to be backed by additional gold and silver reserves. The result was the gradual dying out of private bank-note issuance by the country banks and an effective monopoly for the Bank of England on the printing of new notes.[94]

However, importantly, the Act exempted demand deposits – the accounting entries that banks made either when people deposited money with them or, more likely, were created as a result of borrowing – from the legal requirement of the 100 per cent gold reserve backing. We have seen how fractional reserve banking allowed banks to lend multiples of the amount of gold in their vaults. Similarly, they could create new bank deposits through lending or purchasing assets, which are multiples of the amount of (now restricted) banknotes. Because these account balances were technically a promise by the bank to pay the depositor, they were not restricted by the Act in the same way that banknotes were. This meant that the country banks were able to create them without breaking counterfeiting laws.

Another reason that the 1844 Act did not incorporate demand deposits as part of its legislation is likely the fact that it would be very difficult for any customer or state regulator to be able to tell the difference between a fictitious demand deposit created by the banks when they issue a loan and a 'real' demand deposit placed at a bank by a customer who, for example, has just received their salary. Both types of money will look exactly the same in the banks accounting reports. As Werner suggests:

> *As banks work as the accountants of record – while the rest of the economy assumes they are honest accountants – it is possible for the banks to increase the money in the accounts of some of us (those who receive a loan), by simply altering the figures. Nobody else will notice, because agents cannot distinguish between money that had actually been saved and deposited and money that has been created 'out of nothing' by the bank.*[95]

No doubt also the failure to include demand deposits in the 1844 Act was related to the strength of the commodity theory of money (Section 2.2) at the time, a fact manifested in the rhetoric of the Bullionist school. The paper notes issued by the country banks were much more tangible than their demand deposits and more obviously competitors with commodity money (gold and silver). Railing against paper money, Bullionist William Cobbett argues:

We see the country abounding with paper money; we see every man's hand full of it; we frequently talk of it as a strange thing, and a great evil; but never do we inquire into the cause of it. There are few of you who cannot remember the time when there was scarcely ever seen a bank note among Tradesman and Farmers ... If you look back, and take a little time to think, you will trace the gradual increase of paper money and the like decrease of gold and silver money ...[96]

It was not long before the country banks, no longer able to issue their own private banknotes, began to specialise in deposit taking and the issuing of cheques or account statements.[97] These cheques and statements could be redeemed for Bank of England notes or gold in just the same way as the old banknotes had been. As the Federal Reserve Bank of Chicago puts it:

Transaction deposits are the modern counterpart of banknotes. It was a small step from printing notes to making book-entries crediting deposits of borrowers, which the borrowers in turn could 'spend' by writing checks, thereby 'printing' their own money.[98]

The result was that the 1844 Act failed to stop fractional reserve banking – the creation of new money by private banks. It merely led to a financial innovation in the medium of exchange. At the same time it made the ability of banks to create money out of nothing far less visible: while it is still obvious in Scotland and Northern Ireland, where banks continue to issue paper money, the general public in England and Wales has no daily reminder of the banks' role as the suppliers of the money supply. This has served to perpetuate the myth – widespread even today – that only the central bank or possibly the government creates money.

Whilst the 1844 Act is widely considered to be a key ingredient of the Golden Period of UK financial history over the next 70 years, it was not very effective in preventing banking crises in the remainder of the nineteenth century. Indeed, the act was repeatedly repealed – in 1847, 1857, and 1866 – to allow the Bank of England to print new notes in excess of its gold reserves to prevent massive financial collapses following bank failures.

Many historians attribute the Golden Period not so much to the 1844 Act as to Britain becoming the dominant world power. This underpinned the credibility of the Bank of England's governance of the whole international monetary system through Sterling as the world's reserve currency. It had the additional feature that the British state increasingly came to rely on issuing bonds at interest, just as the United States has been able to do through most of the twentieth century.

2.6. Twentieth century: the decline of gold, deregulation, and the rise of digital money

2.6.1. A brief history of exchange rate regimes (see also Section 4.6.1)

Historically, during the long phase of 'commodity-money', the exchange rate would depend upon the amount of gold, silver, or copper contained in the coins of each country. A coin containing ten grams of gold would exchange for two coins containing five grams of gold, and so on.

Similarly, after the advent of paper money and the gold standard, the exchange rate depended upon the amount of gold a government promised to pay the holder of bank notes. These amounts did not vary greatly in the short-term, and as such exchange rates between currencies were relatively stable. Consequently those who traded across currencies faced little risk that movements in exchange rates would affect their profits, meaning that there was less opportunity for currency speculation and less requirement for 'hedging' against the risk of an exchange rate changing.

2.6.2. WWI, the abandonment of the gold standard and the regulation of credit

The Golden Period came to an abrupt end with the onset of WWI. The government once again became in desperate need for funds and the 1844 Act was again abandoned with little hesitation. Britain left the gold standard in 1914 by unofficially ceasing specie payments: one could no longer redeem banknotes for gold coins. Following the successful US example, the government instead issued its own money (Bradbury bills, named after the then Secretary to the Treasury, John Bradbury) to raise finance for the war. This direct government money was not borrowed from any bank or investor through bond issuance, and it proved successful in combating the acute banking crisis that followed Britain's declaration of war on Germany in August 1914 and contributed to the war economy. As Davies argues,

> *The cessation of internal gold circulation, then conceived simply as an urgent temporary expedient, thereafter became permanent. Thus ended without fuss or fanfare nearly 700 years of intermittent gold coinage circulation, including a century of the full gold standard, ousted ignominiously by bits of scrappy paper.*[99]

After the war, countries attempted to reinstate the gold standard, believing this would restore stability to the international financial system. The UK fixed the value of sterling to gold at its pre-war level under the Gold Standard Act of

1925, but the public could no longer exchange bank notes for gold coins, only gold bullion.

However, the inter-war gold standard did not last for long. In 1931, following a period of financial upheaval, concerns began to surface about Britain's investments in Europe. By September that year, speculators increasingly presented pounds to the Bank of England in order to convert them into gold. In response to this, with the Bank of England unable to support the pound at its official value, on 19 September 1931 Britain abandoned the gold standard. The pound floated freely once again.[100] Other countries had either already left the gold standard or would do so soon after.[101]

The rigid adherence to the standard, the consequent inability for exchange rates to adjust to reflect changes in international competitiveness and the high interest rates required to defend currencies from speculative attacks have been blamed for deepening the Great Depression, with some studies finding a correlation between the length of countries' adherence to the standard and the severity of the depression in that country.[102,103] It has also been suggested that inter-war instability was in part a result of the shift of power from the pre-war dominance of sterling to the new global reserve currency – the US dollar – and hence the de facto governance of the global financial system passing to the US Federal Reserve, which was unaccustomed to and ill-prepared for such an undertaking.

Following WWII, a 20-year period of relative financial stability ensued in much of the Western world, with the Bretton Woods agreement providing a fixed exchange rate against the US dollar, which in turn was convertible into gold at a fixed price. The system lasted into the 1970s until, just like Britain in 1931, the USA found itself unable to live up to the promise to convert dollars into gold. European commentators accused the USA of abusing the system by simply creating too many dollars, with which US firms then bought European companies and assets. The French government responded by demanding the conversion of its dollar balances into gold. As with the British gold standard, it turned out that the promise to convert into gold worked only as long as it was not acted on. In response to the French 'raid on Fort Knox', US President Nixon cancelled the dollar convertibility into gold. By 1976 all the world's major currencies were allowed to float freely against each other.

As with the earlier Golden Period, where the UK's well-established currency and institutions were associated with international stability, it was the institutional structures and macroeconomic context of the immediate post-war period that underpinned the stability of currencies rather than the US retention of a gold standard of $35 an ounce. Importantly during this period there were strict credit controls placed on banks in many Western states. Britain was no different. Banks were required to hold 8 per cent of their assets in the form of cash and a more general liquidity reserve ratio of 28–32 per cent was imposed.[104]

But even this was not seen as enough control at the time. Britain's central bank developed its own qualitative and quantitative credit controls. Known as 'moral suasion', this informal guidance of bank credit by the central bank limited the total amount of credit banks could create, and set quotas for specific sectors. As reported in a review of monetary policy in the 1960s:

> *For much of the ten-year period [the 1960s] the circumstances required more severe restraint on credit than could be achieved by acting on liquidity and ratios. It was therefore necessary to have recourse to direct forms of control – the imposition of lending ceilings. Direct requests to the deposit banks to restrict the level of their advances had been made at times in the 1950s … [T]he terms of the request were fairly general (… that the recent rate of increase in advances should be greatly reduced). Lending ceilings were re-imposed in 1965 when all banks and hire purchase finance houses were asked to restrict their lending to an annual rate of increase of 5 per cent in the twelve months to March 1966. Specific ceilings of this general kind have been in force for most of the time since then. The quantitative ceilings have been accompanied by qualitative guidance – again not a new development – on the direction of lending. This guidance has always accorded priority to export finance.*[105]

As we can see from Figure 6, during this period there was something of a balance between the amount of money in circulation issued by the state in the form of notes, coins and bank-money (it was about 50/50). Such 'window guidance' bank credit controls were abandoned in the early 1970s. As Figure 6 shows, that is when bank credit began to increase rapidly.

2.6.3. Deregulation of the banking sector in the 1970s and 1980s

The period from the late 1960s until the present day saw the gradual deregulation of banking and credit both on an international (Chapter 4) and national scale. Much of the theoretical support for such deregulation was based on an analysis that thought of banks as mere financial intermediaries, as in described in Chapter 1, Section 1.3, and neglecting their crucial function as creators of the money supply.

Figure 6: M4 (broad money) against base money (notes and coins and central bank reserves), 1963–2011 Figure 1: UK money supply, 1963–2011.

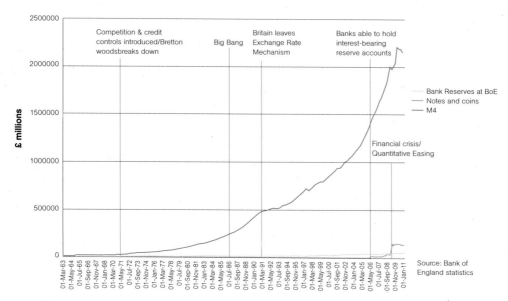

A range of new actors, in particular foreign banks, 'fringe' or 'secondary' banks[*] and hire purchase houses entered the UK financial markets and began lending aggressively. Hire purchase houses, which were not regulated as banks by the Bank of England, provided enormous amounts of credit for the purchase of consumer durables, in particular motor vehicles, which were thought to be highly inflationary.[106] These institutions were not classified as banks and as such were not subject to the credit controls that were only applied to the big clearing banks of the day.

In response, in 1971, the government introduced the Competition and Credit Control (CCC) reforms, which replaced the 8 per cent cash reserve ratio and 28 per cent liquidity reserve ratio with a new 12.5 per cent liquidity reserve ratio.[†] At the same time, however, the Bank brought a much wider range of financial institutions into the remit of banking regulation – previously only the large clearing banks had been included. It also permitted clearing banks to engage freely in the fast-growing 'wholesale' money markets (Box 4) where financial instruments such as government and commercial bonds were traded; previously they had only been able to trade in this through finance house

---

[*] Fringe banks – or secondary banks – were individual small lenders who were not subject to banking regulations – see Reid, M. (1978). The secondary banking crisis – five years on. *The Banker* 128(634): 21–30.

[†] Davies (2005) *op. cit.* p. 409. 12.5 per cent of banks deposits would have to be held in the form of 'eligible reserve assets', which included balances in the Bank of England, Treasury bills and money at call with the discount markets.

Box 4: Wholesale money markets

The term **'money market'** covers the vast network of deals involving the lending and borrowing of liquid assets in a range of currencies, generally between financial institutions such as banks, as well as non-financial companies and the government. These assets include **tradable securities**, such as government securities, Treasury bills or corporate IOUs (commercial paper, or 'CPs'), bank debt (certificates of deposit, 'CDs') usually maturing within a year or less.

'Wholesale' means funds borrowed or lent by those financial institutions in large quantities, rather than the smaller amounts dealt in by private individuals.

---

subsidiaries or 'discount houses'. This also meant that banks could now access central bank money and cash from the money market rather than being dependent on the central bank itself to access central bank reserves and sterling.

As Davies suggests, the Competition and Control reforms saw a fundamental shift in emphasis from the central bank which:

> *changed from rationing bank credit through quantitative ceilings on bank advances and qualitative or selective guidance… to rely on the more generally pervasive influence of the price mechanism, with variation in the rate of interest becoming the main weapon.*[108]

The Bank abandoned its age-old Bank Rate and replaced it with a Minimum Lending Rate (MLR), now described as the Policy Rate or short-term interest rate, which determined the rate at which banks and other financial institutions could access cash and Bank of England reserves.[109] These organisations could then lend reserves to other banks at whatever rate they wanted. Hence monetary regulation became more subject to market forces and the goal of the bank turned to attempting to ensure the market rate of interest was reasonably close to the policy rate.[110]

In 1979, exchange controls which prevented any but authorised UK banks engaging in foreign exchange were lifted and, with the Bretton Woods fixed exchange rate system having been abandoned, as a result there was an explosion in international capital flows in and out of the UK. The UK became an international centre for foreign exchange with a flood of foreign banks opening up in London and the growth of the 'euro-dollar' market which had begun to develop in the 1960s.*

---

*   Davies (2005) *op. cit.* p. 414. Eurodollars is the generic name for US dollar deposits held by non-US banks outside the USA and therefore outside the jurisdiction of the US Federal Reserve. This market developed from the combination of the status of the US dollar as the global reserve currency after WWII, and the desire of the Soviet Union to move its holdings out of the USA during the Cold War.

The oil crises of the 1970s and rapid inflation helped usher into power the free-market-oriented governments of Margaret Thatcher and Ronald Reagan in the UK and USA, respectively, who, influenced by neoclassical free-market economics, began to further dismantle state controls on bank credit, including interest-rate caps. UK Conservative finance ministers Geoffrey Howe and Nigel Lawson oversaw the abolition of all controls over consumer credit together with the deregulation of housing finance in the 'Big Bang' reforms of 1986.[111] Compulsory liquidity reserve ratios were gradually reduced from the 12.5 per cent set in 1971, until eventually they were made voluntary (Figure 7).

A review of the arguments at the time makes clear that the theoretical support for such deregulation was based on the unrealistic assumptions of neoclassical

Figure 7: Decline in UK liquidity reserve ratios.[107]

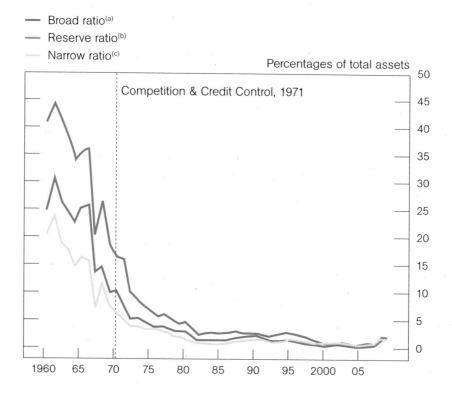

— Broad ratio[(a)]
— Reserve ratio[(b)]
— Narrow ratio[(c)]

Percentages of total assets

Competition & Credit Control, 1971

Sources: Bank of England, Bankers Magazine (1960-68) and Bank calculations. Data before 1967 cover only the London clearing banks.

(a) Cash + Bank of England balances + money at call + eligible bills + UK gifts.

(b) Bank of England balances + money at call + eligible bills.

(c) Cash + Bank of England balances + eligible bills.

theoretical economics, in which banks also perform no unique function, are classified as mere financial intermediaries just like stockbrokers, and which, in particular, does not recognise their pivotal role in the economy as the creators of the money supply. As a consequence, no regulator has since monitored explicitly the quantity of credit created by banks, and the qualitative allocation and direction of these new money injections. There is no monitoring of whether newly created credit is used for transactions that contribute directly to GDP or not. Credit financing trading in existing assets, real or financial, does not contribute to GDP, but instead it contributes to unsustainable asset inflation. Neither is there oversight of whether credit contributing to GDP is used for productive or consumption transactions (the latter creating more direct inflationary pressure).[112]

The globalisation of capital flows and banking services saw a shift towards an international regime of banking regulation with policy being developed by the Basel Committee on Banking Supervision, whose secretariat is located at the Bank of International Settlements (BIS) based in Basel, Switzerland. Many observers consider the Basel Committee as being strongly influenced by the goals of the largest banks in the industrialised countries. Rather than focusing on liquidity, the Basel agreements (I, II, and more recently III) placed emphasis on 'capital adequacy ratios' (Chapter 5).

2.6.5. *The emergence of digital money*

Just as important to our understanding of the modern monetary and banking system, however, have been developments in information and communication technology. These have changed not just the medium of exchange (from cash to cheques to debit and credit cards to internet banking) but the relative power of different actors in relation to the issuance of new money. As cash became less and less important as a medium of payment in relation to demand deposits that could easily be moved around with the use of debit cards or electronic transfers, so the macroeconomic importance of the banking system as the main creator of new money in the economy increased.[113] As the European central bank stated in 2000:

> *At the beginning of the 20th century almost the totality of retail payments were made in central bank money. Over time, this monopoly came to be shared with commercial banks, when deposits and their transfer via checks and giros became widely accepted. Banknotes and commercial bank money became fully interchangeable payment media that customers could use according to their needs. While transaction costs in commercial bank money were shrinking, cashless payment instruments became increasingly used, at the expense of banknotes.[114]*

Today virtually all (most estimates are between 97 to 98 per cent) money in circulation is commercial bank money.[115] As shown in Figure 6, its growth has been exponential. As recently as 1982, the ratio of coins and notes to bank deposits was 1:12 – by 2010 this ratio had risen to 1:37.*

These figures and Figure 6 may appear to run counter to our everyday lived experience of using money. Most people, for example, have probably not noticed a decline in their use of cash over this period – we all still feel more comfortable going out with a tenner in our wallets. But it is important to distinguish between the frequency of transactions and the value of transactions paid for with each type of money. Cash is still used for what numerically is the majority of transactions, but the majority of transactions are very small, for example, less than £10. Digital money – in the form of the moving of demand deposits (bank-money) from one account to another – is used almost exclusively for larger transactions. This is because of the convenience of credit and debit cards and, increasingly, online banking where the volumes are considerably larger. None of these media of exchange involve state-money (notes and coins).

We have discussed how all money is credit. Nowadays, we can also say that, with the exception of a tiny fraction of cash, money is basically information. Huge volumes of money are moved around our economies simply by people typing data into computers. The 1s and 0s, the binary language of the computer, are the closest representation we have to what money is today. Money has never been a commodity, as we have seen, but in our digital world it is now even less tangible than it has ever been. Those with the power to create new money have enormous power – they can create wealth simply by typing figures into a computer, and they decide who can use it, for which purpose.

Let us now examine in detail how this happens in the UK today.

---

* Bank of England statistics: M4 (LPQAUYN) and Notes and Coins (LPMB8H4). Ratio calculated by dividing M4 by Notes and Coins for March 1982 and December 2010 .

3. Money and banking today: Liquidity, payments and solvency

> *Few phrases have ever been endowed with such mystery as open-market operations, the Bank Rate, the rediscount rate. This is because economists and bankers have been proud of their access to knowledge that even the most percipient of other citizens believe beyond their intelligence.*
>
> J.K. Galbraith (1975)[116]

We have now critically examined the common public and textbook understanding of money and banking and showed how banking in the UK has developed over the past three centuries. We have seen that today the bulk of the UK's money supply is created not by the state, the Bank of England, the Treasury, or the Royal Mint, but by a collection of private, profit-oriented companies that are commonly known as banks.

These are the fundamentals. However, it is important also to have a grasp of the workings of the present-day money and banking system in the UK. In particular, we need to understand that there are some constraints on the quantity of credit that banks can create even though they effectively have a licence to create new money.

The next two chapters provide a detailed overview of the way that commercial banking works today in the UK and how it interacts with the central bank, the payment system, and the money markets. To start, we need to address the concept of liquidity.

3.1. Liquidity, Goodhart's law, and the problem of defining money

In Section 2.1, we saw that acceptability as a means of exchange and of final settlement were key functions of money. History suggests that one useful way of judging acceptability of money is whether you can use it to pay taxes and, more generally across the economy, to buy goods and services. However, when defining money mainly as private sector assets, there is not a sharp dividing line between money and non-money. There are some assets which can be much

Figure 8: Liquidity scale.

Cash & central bank reserves — Most liquid

Government bonds

Commercial bonds — Declining liquidity

Mortgage-backed securities — Less liquid

more easily converted into money than others; this quality is referred to as liquidity. More liquid assets are those that can be more certainly realisable at short notice without loss.

For example, my house is very illiquid because I am unlikely to be able to sell it quickly (unless perhaps I offer it for sale at a huge discount), but if I can find a pawnbroker then I can quickly convert my watch into cash. If other people realise that my watch is quite a liquid asset, they might even accept it in exchange for selling me something, because they know they can easily convert it into cash. In this case, my watch has taken on some of the functions of money – we might call this 'near-money'. Because liquidity changes gradually across different assets (i.e. there is a spectrum of liquidity – Figure 8), drawing a line at any particular point will always to a certain extent seem arbitrary.[117]

Banknotes are the most liquid asset, and can be used immediately to perform economic actions like buying, selling, or paying debts, thus meeting immediate wants and needs. Central bank reserves, which function as electronic banknotes for commercial banks trading with one another, are equally liquid.

To this we can add commercial bank money, the electronic money in my bank account, because with electronic banking and debit cards my bank deposits are certainly widely accepted. Indeed bank deposits are sometimes more acceptable since it is actually easier and more convenient to use electronic payment for many routine obligations, including utility bills and taxes, than it is to use cash.

As far as the deposit holder is concerned, electronic money appears to be just as liquid as cash, even if, technically, it isn't.

This seems straightforward for current accounts, or 'demand deposits', but what about savings accounts, or 'time deposits'? An instant-access savings account is really just as liquid as a current account. But what if I have to give seven days' notice? This particular bank deposit is less liquid, but once I have given the bank notice it will be transformed into a more liquid deposit in my current account. This helps explain why the Bank of England uses several different measures of money supply, which are set out below in a simplified form:

Central bank money (also known as M0, high-powered money, monetary base, or narrow money)

1. Notes and coins in circulation (sometimes referred to as cash).

2. Reserve balances at the Bank of England.

Broad money

M1 Notes and coins in circulation with the non-bank public plus sterling current accounts.

M2 M1 plus sterling time deposits with up to three months' notice, or up to two years' fixed maturity.

M3 M2 plus repurchase agreements, money market fund units, and debt securities up to two years – estimated by the European central bank (ECB) for the UK to be consistent with the M3 measure used by the ECB for the euro area.

M4 M3 plus other deposits at UK banks or building societies.

Further complications arise from the capacity of modern capitalism to continuously create new forms of credit/debt that are not perfectly liquid.[118,119] Economist Charles Goodhart argued that defining money was inherently problematic because whenever a particular instrument or asset was publicly defined as money by an authority in order to better control it, substitutes were produced for the purposes of evasion.[*,120] We revisit the question of where to draw the line around 'money' later in Chapters 5 and 6.

---

* Known as 'Goodhart's law'. Goodhart, C.A.E. (1989). *Money, Information and Uncertainty*. London: Macmillan, p. 100.

The process of defining money becomes easier when we focus on the question of when and how new money is created. Then the definitional problems become irrelevant. When a bank makes a loan it invariably credits the borrower's current account, and from there the money is spent. When a bank grants an overdraft facility, it promises that it will make payments on my behalf even though I have no deposits. In this case, new deposits are created for the person to whom I have made a payment. Thus new commercial bank money enters circulation when people spend the credit that has been granted to them by banks (Section 3.2).

Others also sometimes point out that commercial bank money is credit, and then proceed to distinguish this from 'money' and measures of the money supply. Such an argument is mere smoke and mirrors – it is impossible for anyone else to distinguish between a balance on my current account that got there because I paid in £1,000 in cash over the counter, and the same balance that got there because the bank advanced me a £1,000 loan. And even the cash I pay in over the counter had to be withdrawn from another bank account, which may have been funded by a loan or an overdraft. In any event, as the opinion polls referred to in Chapter 1 demonstrate, if you stopped someone in the street and told them that the balance in their current account was not actually money at all, they might well think you had taken leave of your senses.

The Bank of International Settlements describes it as follows:

> *Contemporary monetary systems are based on the mutually reinforcing roles of central bank money and commercial bank monies. What makes a currency unique in character and distinct from other currencies is that its different forms (central bank money and commercial bank monies) are used interchangeably by the public in making payments, not least because they are convertible at par.* [121]

In the next sections, we go through the credit creation process by private banks and the relationship between private banks, the central bank and the payment system.

3.2. Banks as the creators of money as credit

A customer, whom we'll call Robert, walks into a branch of Barclays Bank and asks to borrow £10,000 for home improvements. Barclays makes a cursory check of Robert's income and checks his credit rating, and decides that he can be relied upon to keep up repayments on the loan.

Robert signs a loan contract promising to repay the £10,000, plus the interest, over the next three years, according to an agreed monthly schedule. This loan contract legally binds Robert to make repayments to the bank. As such, it has a value of £10,000 (plus the interest) to the bank. Upon signing, Barclays records it as an asset on its balance sheet (Figure 9):

Figure 9: Loan by Barclays Bank.

BARCLAYS BANK BALANCE SHEET (Step 1)	
Assets (What the borrowers owe to bank + bank's money)	**Liabilities** (What the bank owes to the depositors + bank's net worth)
Loan to Robert: £10,000	

Of course, double entry bookkeeping (Box 5) requires an equal and opposite accounting entry, and besides, Robert now wishes to get access to the money. So Barclays creates a new bank account for him, and gives it a balance of £10,000. This account is a liability of the bank to Robert, so it is recorded on the liabilities side of Barclays' balance sheet (Figure 10):

Figure 10: Bank simultaneously creates a loan (asset) and a deposit (liability).

BARCLAYS BANK BALANCE SHEET (Step 2)	
Assets (What the borrowers owe to bank + bank's money)	**Liabilities** (What the bank owes to the depositors + bank's net worth)
Loan to Robert: £10,000	Robert's new account: £10,000

Note that the bank has expanded its balance sheet and all it has done is added some numbers to a record in a computer database, recording that it has a liability to Robert and also an asset in the form of Robert's agreement to repay his loan. This is the process of extending credit or, more accurately, of creating credit. This credit authorises Robert to make payments of up to £10,000 from this account, using his debit card, cheque book, or bank transfer. The numbers that the bank typed into Robert's account can be used to make payments, and therefore function as money. The process of creating commercial bank money

---

Box 5: Double-entry bookkeeping and T-accounts

A double entry bookkeeping system is a set of rules for recording financial information where every transaction changes at least two different ledger accounts.

The name derives from the fact that financial information used to be recorded in books – hence 'bookkeeping' (whereas now it is recorded mainly in computer systems). These books were called ledgers and each transaction was recorded twice as a 'debit' and a 'credit'.

The accounting equation serves as an error detection system: if at any point the sum of debits does not equal the corresponding sum of credits, an error has occurred. It follows that the sum of debits and credits must be equal. Double-entry bookkeeping is not a guarantee that no errors have been made – for example, the wrong nominal ledger account may have been debited or credited, or the entries completely reversed.

On the balance sheet of a bank, the debits and credits are termed assets and liabilities respectively. A bank's capital (or equity) is derived from the accounting equation: Equity = Assets – Liabilities. By convention, it is recorded on the liability side.

In this guide, we use T-accounts to show what banks' balance sheets look like. T-accounts split the bank's assets (conventionally shown on the left) from liabilities (shown on the right). Assets can be thought of legal contracts that entitle the bank to a stream of future income (interest received) in return for payment of an initial sum (principal) which will eventually be recovered by the bank. Liabilities can be considered as a promise to pay a certain sum in the future, which incurs a stream of expenses (interest paid) until that time.

Commercial banks and the Bank of England do not normally use T-accounts but instead list assets first and then liabilities underneath, but we shall use T-accounts as it is easier to compare multiple bank balance sheets (e.g. a commercial and the central bank) using T-accounts next to one another.

– the money that the general public use – is as simple as a customer signing a loan contract, and the bank typing numbers into a new account set up for that customer.

The process is similar if Robert has an overdraft facility, but in this case no new deposit is created in his account. Instead, a new deposit is created for someone else when he makes a payment to them. The overdraft operates as a variable loan of which the borrower can determine the timing and amount within the limit agreed.

When a bank buys securities ('tradable loans') such as a corporate or government bond, it adds the bond to its assets, and increases the company's bank deposits by the corresponding amount. Similarly, the bank creates new money when it buys assets, goods or services on its own account, or pays its staff salaries or bonuses.

These newly created demand deposits represent new spending power – or money – in the economy. It is not spending power that has been taken out of someone else's savings. As shown in Figure 10, Robert is free to spend his 'deposit' however he wants. However, if Robert spends his credit with customers of other banks, then the other banks will come to Barclays asking it to settle with them. This process of settlement is described next. In Chapter 5, we analyse the extent to which the need for central bank reserves and interbank settlement will limit the willingness of banks to create credit or money in the manner just described.

3.3. Payment: using central bank reserves for interbank payment

If you and I both have an account at the same bank, it is a very simple process for me to transfer £500 to you. I simply instruct my bank to do so and it makes an accounting entry on its computer that shows £500 leaving my account and £500 entering your account. There is no need for any cash to be handed over, or any reason to involve the Bank of England. This clearing or payment function within the same bank has, as we saw in Chapter 2, been going on since Babylonian times. All that is required is for some numbers to be typed into a computer (or written on a clay tablet, in former times) and removed from another account.

But what if we bank with different banks as in the example in Figure 11. Given that a demand deposit, as we have seen, is no more than a contract with a promise to pay, how does it get transferred, as a means of final payment, from one bank to another? One option is for me to withdraw £500 in the form of cash and give it to you to pay into your own account. Most of us would find this highly inconvenient.

Principally, there are two ways for banks to get around this problem. The first is for banks to use their accounts with other banks to settle transfers directly, having netted out transactions in opposite directions. This is called 'bilateral settlement'.

An alternative method is for banks to use their accounts with the central bank. The Bank of England has its own clearing system with its own equivalent of demand deposits that have the status of final means of payment, just as cash or legal tender. Just to recap on Section 1.3, we call this type of money **central bank reserves**. Together with currency in the form of notes and coins which is circulating outside the banking sector, this makes up **high-powered money**, also known as **base money, monetary base,** or **central bank money.**

In the same way that you have a bank account with a particular bank, the banks themselves have bank account(s) with the Bank of England called reserve accounts (Figure 11). Just as you must maintain enough balance in your account to ensure all your routine payments go through, so private banks must maintain reserve balances in their Bank of England account in order to enable payments to other private banks requested by customers. (It should be noted that commercial banks have been using central bank reserves as means of settlement with other banks since the 1770s, as discussed in Sections 2.4 and 2.5.)

In Figure 11, Richard makes a payment of £500 to his landlord Stuart. The result, as shown in the simplified graphic, is simply a transfer between their respective banks' reserves accounts (HSBC and Barclays).

The quantity of central bank reserves is determined by the central bank. It adjusts its reserves to try to always ensure that there are enough in the system for commercial banks to access to make the necessary payments to each other. It ensures there is enough 'liquidity' in the clearing system. Commercial banks cannot 'own' central bank reserves in just the same way as you and I cannot

Figure 11: Commercial banks and central bank reserve account with payment.

'own' demand deposits. Instead commercial banks borrow central bank reserves from the central bank to finance their reserves balances. So commercial banks have a liability to the central bank in the form of these loans and the central bank has an asset as it is owed money by the commercial bank (T-chart 1). Alternatively, they can sell securities to the central bank and receive reserves as payment.

T-chart 1: Balance sheet of private banks and central bank showing reserves

Private banks		Central bank	
Assets (what borrowers owe to the bank)	Liabilities (what the bank owes to customers)	Assets	Liabilities
Loans to customers	Deposits of customers	Loans to private banks	Reserve deposits of private banks
Central bank reserves	Loans from central bank		

Now, let us work through our example of Richard paying his landlord Stuart in more detail. Follow the steps in Figure 12 to understand how this payment is made.

After the transaction, HSBC's and Barclays Bank's balance sheets will have changed in the following way:

T-chart 2: private banks balance sheets

HSBC		Barclays	
Assets	Liabilities	Assets	Liabilities
-£500 central bank reserves to Barclays	-£500 (from Richard to Stuart)	+£500 central bank reserves (from HSBC/ Richard)	+£500 (owed to Richard's Landlord)

Central bank reserves, like bank deposits, are not tangible. They are simply numbers on a computer (Box 6). We can see from T-chart 2 that the total amount of reserves in the central bank reserve accounts has not changed by Richard paying his landlord £500; £500 has been taken out of HSBC's reserve

Figure 12: Payment of £500 from Richard to Landlord.

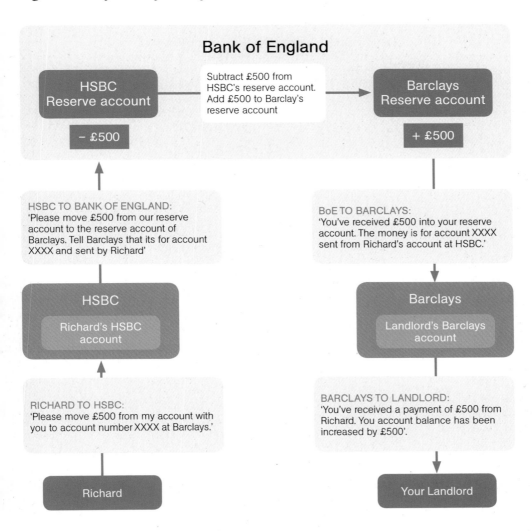

account and £500 has been added to Barclays' account. Barclays receives an increase in its reserves of £500 and also adds £500 to Stuart the Landlord's demand deposits. Again, the accounts are separate but mirror each other.

Box 6: Money as information – electronic money in the Bank of England

A reserve account at the Bank of England is not a physical vault where coins and paper money can be kept. It is just an accounting record in a computer database – in technical terms it is no more complex than a number in an Excel spreadsheet. Central bank reserves refer to the numbers stored in this computer record. Central bank reserves are not tangible, and cannot be stolen in the way that physical cash can. Central bank reserves cost nothing to produce, as one billion can be created in the same length of time that it takes to type out the following numbers: 1,000,000,000.

It is important to appreciate the fact that all money, bar a small amount of paper notes and coins, is no more than a digital record in a computer database. In fact, if you were able to access the database that holds the central bank reserve accounts, it may look like this:

Account Name	Balance
Barclays Plc	£125,352,003,023.54
Lloyds Banking Group	£250,015,135,010.24

The central bank reserves are no more tangible than the £375 billion typed out above. The entire record of balances of the central bank reserve schemes will take up less space on the Bank of England's computer hard drive than the average song on an MP3 player.[*]

So there is no need for any additional money anywhere in the system.

3.3.1. Interbank clearing: reducing the need for central bank reserves

The fact that HSBC's reserves balance has fallen by £500 and Barclays' has risen by £500 could be taken to imply that HSBC needs to replenish its balance, to have sufficient funds for other payments, and Barclays could reduce its balance.

In practice however, there are millions of people across the country all transferring money to each other across only a few major banks (Figure 13). These banks can keep a tally on their computer systems, and usually many of the movements cancel each other out at the end of each day – this is called **intra-day clearing**. Hence the actual amount of central bank reserves that needs to be transferred between banks at the end of the day or overnight (shown in Figure 13 as movements of liquid between the central bank reserve 'buckets') is a small proportion of the total value of the transactions that have taken place between their customers. The larger any individual bank is as a proportion of the total value of customer payments, the fewer reserves

---

[*] The full record of the billions of transactions from and to each account will of course take up many thousands of times more space than the simple record of the total balance.

Figure 13: Simplified diagram of intra-day clearing and overnight trading of central bank reserves between six commercial banks.

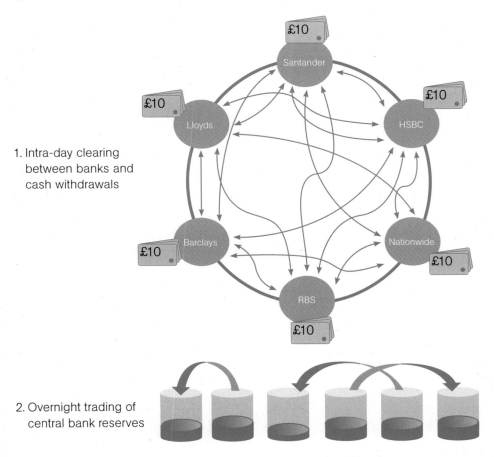

1. Intra-day clearing between banks and cash withdrawals

2. Overnight trading of central bank reserves

it is likely to need because so many transactions take place between its own customers and not between it and the other banks.

For example, just before the financial crisis in 2007, Lloyds Bank (now merged with HBOS and nationalised) had 19 per cent of the personal current account market.[122] That means that 1 in 5 people in the UK banked with Lloyds and so it could clear a significant number of transactions between its own customers with no need for any central bank reserves or without any need to use its balances with other banks. Furthermore, whilst tens of millions of pounds were leaving its accounts every day to go to different banks, so tens of millions would be coming back to it from the same banks. The difference between these inflows and outflows is obviously much smaller than the total gross value of the flows. Hence Lloyds only needed to keep a small proportion of central bank money as a proportion of total payments, conferring a commercial advantage to scale. Other things being equal, the smaller the bank, the relatively larger the amount of central bank reserves it requires to settle its customers' transactions, and so the lower the amount of more profitable assets it will be able to hold.

At the end of each day, commercial banks will either be 'short' of central bank reserves and need to borrow more or they will be 'long' on central bank reserves and have 'excess' liquidity. As in Figure 13, we can imagine banks' reserves with the central bank as buckets with different volumes of liquid. Some banks will have too much and others too little, so they will trade with each other to balance this out in preparation for the following day's trading. To adjust its reserves, a bank can either borrow funds directly from the central bank or, more usually, it will engage in overnight trading with other banks on the Interbank money market. Banks that have excess reserves will typically lend them to banks in need of reserves in return for highly liquid interest-bearing assets, usually gilts (government securities) (see Chapter 2, Box 3 on bond issuance). The rates of interest on loans between banks will typically be better than banks could attain when borrowing directly from the central bank.

If central bank reserves are withdrawn from one account, they must go up in some other account. What this means is that the 46 banks within the clearing system know that there should always be enough money in aggregate to meet all the necessary payments (although there may not be enough reserves to meet a particular reserve requirement, if the central bank imposes such a rule – currently not the case in the UK). This means that if a bank finds itself with too few reserves to make a payment, it can borrow central bank reserves from another bank within the loop, which, by definition, will have excess reserves. And the opposite also applies – if a bank has excess reserves, it can lend these to a bank in need of more reserves. The one vital caveat, as we discuss later, is that banks have enough confidence in one another to be happy to lend to each other.

These transfers are made on the interbank money market (Box 4) at the interbank market rate of interest. We explore how the Bank of England attempts to influence this rate in Chapter 5.

3.3.2. *Effects on the money supply*
Commercial banks can increase or decrease their reserves with the central bank in a number of ways. They can borrow additional reserves from other banks or borrow reserves from the central bank, usually by posting gilts as collateral. The central bank effectively creates such reserves when it lends them to the commercial banks. The banks can also sell securities to the central bank or other banks in exchange for reserves.

Box 7: Real time gross settlement (RTGS)

Forty-six banks currently have reserve accounts with the Bank of England.[123] Around £780 billion of transfers are made on average each day between these reserve accounts.[124] With all 46 reserve accounts, there are a total of 2,070 different payment flows in both directions between the accounts (money can be transferred from each individual bank to every other bank).[*] Rather than each bank having to deal with 45 other banks in order to make payments between them, they can simply send payment instructions to the Bank of England's RTGS (real time gross settlement) processor.

The RTGS, which was established in 1996, is a computer system that stores the balance of each bank's reserve account and the transactions going to and from each reserve account.

The RTGS processor handles the process of transferring the money by reducing the balance of the paying bank's reserve account, and increasing the balance of the receiving bank's reserve account.

RTGS refers to the fact that payments between reserve accounts through the RTGS processor are made instantly, and the full amount of the payment is transferred. This is in contrast to 'multilateral net settlement' systems, whereby transactions between banks are queued, cancelled out as much as possible (i.e. Bank A's payment to Bank B might cancel out another payment that Bank B needs to make to Bank A), and the net difference is transferred at a regular interval (such as every two hours for 'faster payments services', or daily for transfers such as BACS).

Commercial bank money outside the closed loop, however, can be created at will by banks and is destroyed when customers repay their loans. As Keynes argued, if all the banks 'move in step' and all create new loans (which is quite typical during times of economic confidence), the aggregate amount of money (the money supply) will increase in the economy and the central bank may forced to increase the aggregate amount of reserves in the system to ensure the payment system does not collapse.[125] This dynamic is commonly described in academic terminology as an 'endogenous money supply' and will be explored further in Chapter 6.

Conversely, during a downturn, more people will repay their loans than banks are willing to create new ones and the money supply will contract.

3.4. Cash

The Bank of England clearing payment system is a closed loop (Figure 13). As a customer, I cannot withdraw either my bank deposits (in electronic form) or

---

[*] Forty-six banks that can each send payments to 45 other banks, assuming one counts every direction of payment as one 'flow', rather than counting each bilateral relationship as one 'flow' (in which case it would be half as many (1,035).

any central bank reserves. I can, however, withdraw cash, as shown in Figure 13. One of the commercial banks' key functions is to provide cash on demand to customers who have positive balances in their accounts (withdrawals from cash-machines are limited up to £250 a day in the UK).

Where does this cash come from? Just like central bank reserves, it comes from the central bank. To meet customer requests for cash the commercial bank turns some of its central bank reserves into cash. Hence, when a customer withdraws cash the bank's liability falls by the same amount as the fall in its cash holdings (see T-chart 3). A commercial bank's balance sheet will record cash 'holdings' as assets held with the central bank, along with reserves.

T-chart 3: Private and central bank balance sheet

Private banks		Central bank	
Assets	**Liabilities**	**Assets**	**Liabilities**
Loans to customers	Deposits of customers		
central bank reserves and cash holdings	Loans from central bank	Loans to private banks	Reserve deposits of private banks and banknotes issued to banks

As shown in Figure 13, every bank must hold enough cash on its premises to ensure its account holders can get access to it on demand. The need to hold cash on demand thus places a concrete liquidity constraint on banks, but it is a constraint that has become less and less significant as the proportion of cash used for payments in the economy has declined (see Section 2.6).

3.4.1. Is cash a source of 'debt-free' money?

Given that bank notes are still created by the Bank of England, some monetary analysts have concluded that there are two 'money supplies'. Firstly a supply of cash, created by the Bank of England and injected into the economy by being lent to commercial banks, and secondly a much larger supply of bank-created money created as banks make loans to and buy assets from businesses and members of the public. Indeed, as we discussed in Section 3.1, Bank of England statistics do distinguish between cash and the 'broad' money supply (which includes commercial bank money).

However, the reality now is slightly different. While it is true that cash has a different status from bank deposits – as the run on Northern Rock demonstrated, people have more confidence in banknotes – it is only possible for members of the public to get hold of cash via their banks deposits. In this sense one could describe cash as a physical representation of commercial bank money, over which the Bank of England retains the branding rights. The reason for this is as follows. When the Bank of England created bank notes, it does not give them to the government for spending directly into the economy. Instead, it lends them to commercial banks in exchange for either gilts (government bonds) or central bank reserves.

The commercial banks then effectively 'sell' the cash to the public. When you take money out of a cash machine, you are not literally withdrawing that cash from your account. Instead, you are swapping banknotes for the numbers (bank deposits) in your account. From the bank's perspective, they initially had an asset (the £10 note) and a liability to you (recorded as your bank balance). When you take cash out of the ATM, both the bank's assets and liabilities fall by £10, as they hand the cash over to you and reduce the balance of your account by £10 (T-chart 4).

T-chart 4: Withdrawal of £10.00

Private bank A	
Assets	Liabilities
cash holdings = £100	Alex's deposits = £100

Alex withdraws £10.00 cash from the machine

Private bank A	
Assets	Liabilities
cash holdings = £90	Alex's deposits = £90

The significance of this is that members of the public collectively can only access cash if they have commercial-bank money in their accounts, or if they sell assets (e.g. bonds) to the central bank. The only way in which the money supply can be increased by the government or central bank is through the purchase of assets from the non-bank private sector.

> ## Box 8: Seigniorage, cash and bank's 'special profits'
>
> The Bank of England sells bank notes to commercial banks. They sell these notes at face value (a £10 note sells for £10), yet the cost of printing a £10 note is just a few pennies. The difference between the face value and cost of production gives the Bank of England a substantial profit. This profit from the creation of money is known as 'seigniorage', and is paid over to the Treasury, where it can be used to fund government spending or to reduce taxation. In the years 2000 and 2009 this seigniorage amounted to nearly £18 billion.[126]
>
> The growth of digital commercial bank money, vis-à-vis government issued cash, can be seen to have the effect of significantly reducing this seigniorage profit to the government proportionate to the total money supply.[127] Commercial banks do not generate seigniorage themselves as they issue credit which will, at some point, be repaid in full. However, as we discussed in Section 2.4 on Fractional Reserve Banking, commercial banks can be seen to generate 'special profits' from their power to issue money in the form of credit through the interest charged upon loans and used overdraft facilities.
>
> Huber and Robertson suggest the interest charged on the issuance of money by banks can be viewed as a 'money tax', since the government could issue non-interest bearing money directly in to the economy. They also argue that bank's enjoy a form of additional 'special profit' because they don't have to first borrow this money like other organisations. This 'special profit' can be thought as equivalent to the central bank's base rate over the course of the loan.[128]
>
> The total profits arising are then the rate of interest charged on the loan (e.g. 8 per cent), added to the base rate (e.g. 2 per cent) = 10 per cent, minus any interest paid by the bank to the customer on any portions of the loan that the customer has not yet spent. This is opposed to an interest rate 'spread' profit of 8 per cent - 2 per cent = 6 per cent. Using this methodology, Huber and Robertson calculated that in 2000 the 'special profits' generated through this were £21 billion.[129]

3.5. How do banks decide how much central bank money (reserves and cash) they need?

How might banks decide then on how much central bank money to keep aside for payments? Let's run through an example.

Barclays issues Mrs Jones a loan of £10,000. This creates an interest-bearing asset of £10,000. Simultaneously, it creates an interest-bearing deposit for Mrs Jones of £10,000 which she can spend as money.

However, Barclays knows that Mrs Jones may want to convert some of this £10,000 into cash. And also that she may transfer some to other banks electronically which will mean that Barclays will need some additional central bank reserves.

So Barclays could sell some of its liquid assets (government securities) on the money markets, replenishing its stocks of central bank reserves when it receives payment, from other banks, for the assets it sold. By how much? Given that the ratio of physical cash to customer demand deposits in 2010 was 1:37,[130] the bank decides it only needs an additional £270 (£10,000/37) in cash. In addition, since the ratio of central bank reserves to deposits in 2010 was 1:15, it decides to increase its reserve account by £667 (£10,000/15), which requires borrowing the additional reserves on the interbank market. So out of the total loan of £10,000, the bank accesses just £937 of additional central bank money, equivalent to less than 10 per cent of the total loan.[131]

On average, prior to the financial crisis of 2008 onwards, the banks had £1.25 in central bank money for every £100 of customers' money. In the more cautious, post-crisis environment, the banks still have on average only £7.14 for every £100 of customers' money.[132]

3.6. Is commercial bank money as good as central bank money?

Let us revisit briefly the popular conception of banking as a safe-deposit box that we set out in Chapter 1. If you had £500 in your bank account, it might be logical to assume that the bank must have £500 in central bank money, ring-fenced for you, ready to use. But this is not the case. As the customer of a bank, you do not have access to any central bank money any more than there is a bundle of cash with your name on it lying in the vaults. For your £500, as we have seen, the bank will only hold a small proportion of central bank reserves. Like goldsmiths before them, banks know that not many customers are likely at any one time to demand all of their money in cash. It also knows that within the closed loop of the RTGS (Box 7, a lot of payments (and central bank reserves) will be coming back to them as well as leaving.

So your money is not central bank money, it is a 'promise to pay' from a commercial bank. But as we saw in Chapter 2 on the history and nature of money, even central bank money is only a promise to pay that is enforced by the state. The difference between the credibility of central bank money (including cash) and commercial bank money is further blurred by the insurance of commercial bank money by the state.

3.6.1. *Deposit insurance*
Commercial banks are in a rather privileged position compared with ordinary businesses. Not only are they allowed to create money and allocate purchasing power, but someone else guarantees to pay their liabilities for them if they are unable to. That someone else is you, the taxpayer, via the government. As we described in Chapter 1, the Financial Services Compensation Scheme (FSCS)

guarantees that the first £85,000 of any money deposited in UK licensed banks will be repaid if they are unable to take the payment. This £85,000 is risk-free. It has been transformed by the state from an IOU issued by a bank to an IOU issued by the government. For any deposit above £85,000, if the bank went into liquidation you would join the queue of creditors hoping to get some of their money back.

So, in summary, your account with a bank provides you with the right to request a transfer to another bank, guaranteed up to £85,000.

These institutional arrangements reinforce the notion that bank credit is money, and because banks can extend credit, they can create money as effectively as when the Bank of England rolls the printing presses to produce more banknotes.

3.7. Managing money: repos, open market operations, and direct supply of reserves

Towards the end of Chapter 2, we discussed how, during the 1970s, a fundamental shift occurred in the way the Bank of England conducted monetary policy. As new kinds of financial institutions – secondary banks – began lending aggressively, the Bank decided that rather than try to regulate the quantity of credit provided by the banking system as a whole, it would attempt to influence the price of credit. The price or cost of credit is the interest rate charged on it when it is lent out. This makes sense in a world of perfect information, complete and competitive markets, flexible prices, zero transactions costs, and utility-maximising agents which are the requirements for market clearing (equilibrium). In such a world, higher interest rates should lead to a reduction in the demand for credit and vice versa, as the credit market, like all markets would be in equilibrium.

Every commercial bank may need to borrow reserves and cash from the central bank. So by changing the rate of interest charged on central bank money, the Bank of England can, in theory, influence the demand for loans from banks, as banks will pass on its interest rate to customers.

Banks access reserves indirectly via the interbank or wholesale market (Box 4) by selling or lending government securities (gilts) (Box 3). Banks lend reserves to each other at the market rate of interest. The closer the market rate of interest is to the policy rate set by the Bank (Bank Rate) the more effectively changes in the Bank Rate will carry through and the more 'reliably monetary policy is implemented' (see also Section 5.3 and Appendix 1.[133]

Figure 14: Open market operations by the Bank of England.

A. Withdrawing liquidity

1. Bank of England sells government bonds to the interbank money market

2. It receives central bank reserves/cash in return, withdrawing reserves from commercial banks' accounts at the central bank reducing liquidity in the system

B. Increasing liquidity

1. Bank of England buys government bonds from the interbank money market

2. It provides central bank reserves/cash in return, increasing reserves at the commercial banks' and increasing liquidity in the system

The central bank cannot directly determine the market rate of interest in the interbank market, but it can affect the market rate of interest by lending and borrowing reserves itself on this market to try and keep this rate close to the policy rate. These loans are conducted via repurchasing agreements (repos), and other open-market operations or through providing 'standing facilities'.

3.7.1. Repos and open market operations

As shown in Figure 14, the central bank may have to make loans to commercial banks to fund their reserve account deposits. The primary objective of the Bank's Open Market Operations (OMOs) is therefore to supply a sufficient quantity of reserves. Nowadays it does this primarily via secured loans or repos, rather than buying or selling government bonds, or gilts, from the banks for cash. Repos are collateralised loans in which the commercial banks have to provide high-quality collateral, such as gilts, in exchange for receiving the loan.* With repos and reverse repos, central banks can add or subtract liquidity from the financial system very quickly and precisely. Nevertheless, they only constitute one example of central bank transactions. In practice, central banks are always engaged in purchase and sale operations, and their true quantitative monetary policy stance can be observed by netting out all their transactions.

In the UK, in normal times (i.e. prior to 2008), the banks decide the quantity of central bank reserves they wish to hold every month to accommodate their payments with other banks.[134] So the central bank knows exactly how much to lend, in aggregate, to the banking system. And these reserves are then distributed between banks via the money market (see Appendix 1 for developments since the financial crisis).

Since the rate charged on the loans is the Monetary Policy Committee's policy rate, and the demand for reserves is met by the supply from the central bank, traded rates in the money market tend to be close to the policy rate. In some instances, however, market rates can deviate from the policy rate. This is usually due to some kind of market friction or loss of confidence or could result from a bank being short of reserves and unable to meet its commitments in the interbank market.

If the central bank believes there is merit in supplying extra liquidity in the interbank market – normally indicated by the interbank rate going significantly above the policy rate – it can make additional loans to the banks, collateralised by government securities, or it can engage in outright asset purchases.

Once it decides that the market no longer needs these extra reserves, it can wait for the loans to mature or it can absorb the excess reserves sooner by selling securities into the market.

The RTGS system (Box 7) requires large stocks of reserve-like assets (i.e. government securities). Hence, its implementation in the late 1990s saw a massive uptake in repos and short-term (overnight) OMOs to ensure that liquidity was maintained. From the perspective of the central bank, when it grants the repo, it is a secured loan, as it is backed by a government security. The government securities given to the central bank as collateral will continue to appear as assets in the balance sheets of commercial banks. An asset of additional central bank reserves will appear with a matching liability to the central bank.

---

* Legally a repo involves the security being sold in exchange for cash with an agreement to resell the security in the other direction at a pre-specified later date, but this effectively implies a collateralised loan.

3.7.2. *Standing facilities*

The Bank of England has a range of facilities designed to help deal with unusual market conditions. For example, it offers standing facilities in which a bank can always lend or borrow additional funds to/from the central bank at a penal rate relative to the policy rate. Typically, the borrowing and lending rates have been 1 per cent above and below the policy rate, respectively.

Lending facilities allow banks to borrow reserves directly from the central bank, again in return for government securities, and **deposit facilities** allow banks to deposit reserves directly with the central bank.[135]

If a commercial bank receives 'new' central bank money, then the aggregate amount of reserves in the system will have increased. With this in mind, the Bank of England will only exchange gilts for central bank reserves in one of two places:

1. The **Operational Lending Facility** exists primarily as a conduit for monetary policy in normal times. It allows commercial banks to exchange gilts for central bank reserves overnight, at a spread of 25 basis points above the Bank Rate. This short-term lending is primarily intended to facilitate borrowing if a bank suffers temporary payment difficulties, or if the interbank overnight rate has become particularly volatile. However, the penal rate and the short-term nature of the lending are designed to ensure that the extra reserves are not used to enable more lending.

2. The **Asset Purchase Facility** (recently referred to as **Quantitative Easing**) allows the central bank to purchase gilts and other types of assets outright, for which it issues newly created central bank reserves. This may help drive down interest rates in asset markets and increase liquidity, with the intention of incentivising banks to begin lending again. But it may also result in more money circulating in the economy, thus stimulating economic activity, even if interest rates remain unchanged. However, the gilts that the Bank of England buys in exchange for reserves are not bought from the government, in order to comply with the Maastricht Treaty, Article 101 (see Section 4.1), although the economic effect is the same when the Bank of England purchases government bonds held by other investors.

As well as exchanging gilts for reserves, the Bank of England also exchanges other assets for gilts through its **Discount Window Facility**.

3.7.3. *Discount Window Facility*

The Discount Window Facility is a permanent facility to provide liquidity insurance to the banking sector. This allows banks to borrow gilts from the Bank of England, in exchange for other less liquid collateral, with the idea being that the banks will then be able to exchange these gilts for central bank reserves on the interbank market. But they have to pay higher fees that reflect the type of collateral and the size of the drawing relative to the size of the borrowing bank. Gilts rather than reserves are supplied, in order not to affect the amount of central bank reserves available to the banking sector as a whole.

3.8. Managing money: solvency and capital

We have so far explored how banks and the central bank try to ensure there is sufficient liquidity in the banking system. Liquidity involves the ability to be able to meet demand for withdrawals when many people want to withdraw money at the same time. In contrast, solvency is the long-term stability of a bank's finances, and is related to its capital.

Capital can be in the form of equity, or 'own funds', which constitutes the initial investment by shareholders plus retained profits. It also includes additional equity issued to investors over time (Figure 15). Because it can use retained profits as capital, every time a bank makes a profit, it can set some aside to increase its capital. Capital also contains a third component: provisions. These cover principally depreciation and amortisation (which are typically reported as negative entries on the asset side) and bad loans. They are a substantial component of capital. Between 2004 and 2010 they constituted virtually the whole of UK banks' retained earnings (which includes retained profits): £159.6 billion out of £160 billion. Only the retained profits portion, earnings after provisions, is equity capital.

The equity capital proportion of capital is a liability of the bank to itself or its shareholders. In contrast to deposits it cannot be drawn down by its owners. Instead, the own funds are reduced when a borrower defaults on a loan. In that case, the same amount would be reduced from loans on the asset-side (as the loans default) and the 'own capital' on the liability side (Figure 15). When there is too large a proportion of bad loans, own capital – that is, the net worth of the bank – can become negative. In this case, the bank becomes insolvent. This can happen easily, since capital is commonly less than 10 per cent of bank assets. This means that a mere 10 per cent fall in values of assets held by banks will wipe out most banks.

Figure 15: Balance sheet for commercial bank including capital.

BALANCE SHEET FOR COMMERCIAL BANK	
Assets £	**Liabilities £**
Loans to customers	Customers deposits
Reserves at the BoE	
Cash	
Financial assets (e.g. government securities)	Loans from other financial institutions
Other assets (e.g. buildings, investments)	Capital Equity capital:
	• share capital
	• retained profits
	Provisions
	Subordinated debt (liability to bondholders)
TOTAL LIABILITIES = TOTAL ASSETS	

Another way of putting this is that the own capital shows what would be left over for shareholders if the bank was wound up and all its assets used to pay off all its liabilities. This is relevant because if a bank goes bankrupt, its creditors (those with claims to the bank's liabilities) take precedence over its equity holders, who are last in the queue.

Capital can also include liabilities that are, for regulatory purposes, allowed to be substituted for equity capital, such as subordinated (long-term) debt. Subordinated debt is the liability banks owe to the purchasers of their bonds, who have accepted the risk that if a bank falls into difficulty it may default on its bonds which may therefore become worthless.

The most recent international regulations (Basel III) incorporate subordinated debt as an allowable form of capital (Chapter 5). Note that capital does not represent a physical pool of cash, as the funds are in practice invested. It is an entirely different concept from liquidity.

- Solvency is determined by whether you have sufficient capital to cover losses on your assets.

- Liquidity is determined by whether you have sufficient liquid assets to meet your liabilities.

This said, a lack of liquidity can cause a bank to become technically insolvent. In an attempt to convert its assets into cash, the bank might have to sell them at such a discount that its losses exceed its capital.

3.9. Summary: liquidity and capital constraints on money creation

So in summary, there are two main liquidity constraints on the creation of new commercial bank money that may affect individual banks:

1. Having enough central bank reserves to ensure cheque, debit card or online payments can be made to other banks in the Bank of England closed-loop clearing system at any one time. Individual banks have a number of ways of boosting the reserve balances, including borrowing from other banks on the interbank market.[*]

2. Keeping enough of their demand deposits in the form of cash so that solvent customers can get access to cash whenever they wish.

In practice these constraints are weak under the current monetary policy regime as we explain in Chapter 5. Every bank also has a capital constraint – it must ensure it has enough own funds so that if customers' default on their loans, it can absorb these losses without threatening the bank's solvency. However, in aggregate, banks are not constrained by capital, as they create the money that circulates and can be used to increase capital.

This chapter concludes our exploration of the mechanics of the modern banking system. We return to the questions of how the system is regulated in Chapter 5, and consider further how the Bank of England seeks to influence the creation of new money by commercial banks.

But first, to complete our account of money and banking today, we examine two further important elements of the system – the role of the government in spending and taxing money (fiscal policy), and the role of foreign exchange.

---

[*] See Goodhart, C.A.E. (1989). *Money, Information and Uncertainty*. London: Macmillan; and Werner, R. (2005). *New Paradigms in Macroeconomics*. Basingstoke: Palgrave Macmillan.

4. MONEY AND BANKING TODAY: GOVERNMENT FINANCE AND FOREIGN EXCHANGE

This chapter reviews the role of the government and international dynamics in the modern monetary system. We saw in Chapter 2 the vital role of the state in determining the unit of account and creating demand for a currency through taxation and how, through bond issuance, it developed the capacity to borrow money from banks. This chapter lays out how these activities – often described as 'fiscal policy' – are conducted today, and how the government's accounts actually work. We also examine the effect of government spending and borrowing on the money supply, including the debate around 'crowding out', and the role of foreign exchange, with greater detail in Appendix 4. We begin, however, with an analysis of the legal limits placed upon the government in terms of its power of money creation by the UK's membership of the European Union.

4.1. The European Union and restrictions on government money creation

As we have seen, in the UK it is commercial banks that create new money and not the government.* As explained in Section 3.4, even cash, which is physically 'created' by the Bank of England, cannot, under normal conditions, enter circulation without customers first exchanging it for digital bank money.

How did this situation come about? The Treaty of Maastricht, signed on 7 February 1992, created the European Union and led to the creation of the ECB, and the introduction of a single currency, the euro from 2002. The Treaty, along with its subsequent revisions, specifies a set of economic and monetary rules which all members are obliged to adhere to, including the UK, even though it is not in the euro zone. This includes the statutory independence of the ECB from any government or democratically elected parliament.

---

* Advocates of 'neo-Chartalism' and 'Modern Monetary Theory' (MMT) might disagree. They have argued that governments create money and then spend it into the economy, with taxes a means to create a demand for the currency – see, for example, Wray (1998) *op. cit.* Chapter 3; Mosler (2010) *op. cit.* However, MMT takes the USA's institutional monetary arrangements as standard and it is less clear that they apply to the European setting where we have a separate and legally independent central bank, as specified in the Maastricht Treaty. For a critique see Febrero Eladio (2009) *op. cit.* pp. 523–541.

One of the most important rules of the Treaty in relation to money creation is Article 101 EC (now known as Article 126 of the Treaty on the Functioning of the European Union (TFEU)).* This prohibits the direct financing of government spending by the nation's central bank. This includes any overdraft or credit facility and the direct purchase of any debt instrument (i.e. gilts, treasury bonds) by the central bank. Article 101 EC does however allow the central bank to purchase debt instruments on the secondary market, i.e. after they have previously been issued to private investors and started to be traded in the money markets (see Chapter 2, Box 4).

This is exactly what the UK central bank did during the financial crisis of 2007/2008. During the period of what was called 'quantitative easing', the Bank of England did not create new money in the sense of new purchasing power in the economy, as is often thought. Rather, it pumped vast quantities of central bank reserves into the banking system via the purchase of government bonds (gilts) on the secondary market. It did not, and is not permitted to under Article 101 EC, purchase newly issued gilts directly from the UK government. Such an action would, of course, provide the government with newly created money which could be spent directly into the economy via government departments or used to reduce national debt.

The ECB has followed a similar course of action in the eurozone more recently by buying €45 billion of Greek bonds and more recently Irish, Portuguese, Spanish, and Italian bonds from the secondary market in an attempt to prevent a loss of confidence in the European sovereign debt bond markets.[136,137]

These EU rules ensure that when government spending exceeds taxes, governments are forced to borrow funds from the market and run up a deficit, rather than finance the deficit or increase public spending through new central bank money creation. This is why the interest rates on government debt of different European countries, particularly since the financial crisis, are the focus of so much media attention. If the interest rates on government debt reach a certain level, the markets may lose confidence in the government's capacity to ever repay its loans, or roll over its debt, pushing interest rates even higher until eventually the country faces the prospect of default. As political economist Geoffrey Ingham argues, the Maastricht Treaty effectively removed the power of money creation from individual states and subjected them to market discipline:

---

* Consolidated Version of the Treaty on the Functioning of the European Union. Retrievable from http://eur-lex.europa.eu/LexUriServ/LexUriServ.do?uri=OJ:C:2008:115:0047:0199:EN:PDF [accessed 14 June 2011). The treaty also forbids governments privileged access to financial institutions (Article 102). Following the Lisbon Treaty of 2009, Article 101 EC was revised and is now known as Article 126 of the Treaty on the Functioning of the European Union, abbreviation TFEU or TEU. There were no substantive changes to policy however. For tables of equivalence see: http://eur-lex.europa.eu/en/treaties/index.htm

Box 9: Could the government directly create money itself?

There are many historical examples of governments funding fiscal shortfalls through the issuance of government money. This was done in the UK during WWI, and prior to this via the elaborate system of tally sticks deployed between the eleventh and nineteenth centuries[139] (Section 2.3) Similarly, the governments of Germany, Japan, and the USA issued at times significant amounts of government money, mainly during the nineteenth century.[140]

While the issuance of government money to fund fiscal expenditure is often thought to be inflationary, this need not be the case, especially if limited by the amount of money-supply expansion needed to reach the growth potential of the economy. As has been argued by Huber and Robertson[141] and others, government-created money may represent an efficient use of the monetary system to minimise the tax burden and maximise value for tax-payers. No servicing costs in the form of interest and interest on interest (compound interest) are incurred. This could be a substantial benefit at a time when many a government spends as much or even more on compounded interest on their debts than on their core government expenditure programmes (see also Box 8 on 'seigniorage'). Exploring alternative methods of creating new money is beyond the scope of this book, but these historical examples are important to illustrate that alternative systems are not just possible but have been tested and been effective.

The latter constraint [article 101] is aimed at preventing individual states from monetizing their debt, in the time-honoured fashion, which would compromise the ECB's [European central bank's] absolute control of the production of money. Now that individual member central banks cannot monetize their states' debts, budget deficits must be financed directly in the money market – like those of any private corporation.[138]

These restrictions on credit creation do not apply to 'publicly owned credit institutions' which have full credit creation powers and are treated in exactly the same way as private banks by the central bank. Furthermore, as the European sovereign debt crisis unfolded, the ECB has interpreted some of the rules 'flexibly', so that its credibility and enforceability in case of non-compliance by a member government are now somewhat more doubtful. Finally, as will be discussed below, these rules do not prevent the government borrowing from commercial banks which in turn will create new money, to fund the public sector borrowing requirement.

4.2. Government bank accounts

How does the government then 'spend'? Like me and you, and unlike commercial banks, in order to spend the government first needs to obtain money from somewhere. Generally, this spending is either funded from revenue, proceeds from profitable government-operated enterprises or services, national insurance contributions and taxes, or through borrowing.*

4.2.1. *The Consolidated Fund*

Like any organisation that wishes both to receive and spend money, the government has bank accounts. However, unlike most organisations, the government's primary bank accounts are held at the Bank of England. The oldest of the accounts is the Consolidated Fund (CF) (Figure 16), which was established in 1787 as 'one fund into which shall flow every stream of public revenue and from which shall come the supply for every service.'[142] Administered by HM Treasury, the Consolidated Fund can essentially be thought of as the government's current account. The taxes collected by HM Revenue and Customs (HMRC) are the primary inflows into the Consolidated Fund (Figure 16).† However, if the government is running a deficit, then spending outflows exceed tax inflows. To make the account balance, the difference must be made up through government borrowing.

4.2.2. *The National Loans Fund*

The National Loans Fund (NLF), in collaboration with the Debt Management Office, undertakes borrowing on behalf of the Consolidated Fund and forwards to the Consolidated Fund the funds needed to balance its account each day (Figure 16).

Established in 1968 in order to separate borrowing and lending activities from the Consolidated Fund, the NLF is run by HM Treasury and has its own bank account at the Bank of England. The NLF funds the deficit in various ways:

1. Savings deposited in National Savings and Investments (NS&I) accounts (which, excluding the ordinary account, are liabilities of the National Loans Fund).

2. Borrowing from the money markets through the issuing of sterling denominated government bonds, also known as gilt-edged securities or gilts and Treasury bills.[144] These are sold to the Debt Management Account (DMA) and from there the Debt Management Office sells them into the market (Figure 16).

---

* The government may also raise funds through other means, for example by selling off national industries and assets. These are however all one off payments, and cannot fund a permanent government deficit. The government could also simply print money and use this to fund its expenditure, but as already discussed EU rules prevent this.

† Other smaller inflows include Consolidated Fund Extra Receipts (CFERs) and any repayments from the Contingencies Fund. An example of Consolidated Fund Extra Receipts (CFERs) would be any fines levied which are not retained by the originating department. The Contingencies Fund is a fund used to provide any urgent expenditure or small payments which have not been approved by parliament.

Figure 16: The Exchequer Pyramid – key bodies and relationships involved in government accounts.[143]

HMRC	H.M. Revenue & Customs	DMO	Debt Management Office
OPG	Office of the Paymaster General	DMA	Debt Management Account
NS&I	National Savings & Investments	PWLB	Public Works Loan Board
EFA	Exchequer Funds and Accounts	CRND	Commissioners for the reduction of the National Debt

3. Transferring any surplus unused balances from other government bank accounts.

4. The NLF also receives all the profits from the Issues Department of the Bank of England.[145] The Issues Department is responsible for supplying banknotes. This seigniorage revenue is, of course, a profitable activity, as the cost of producing a banknote is a small fraction of its face value (see Section 3.4, Box 8)

As well as making up any shortfall in the Consolidated Fund, the NLF provides finance to the Debt Management Account and the Exchange Equalisation Account (EEA) (Appendix 3). The NLF also makes loans to public sector bodies as well as providing finance to other government organisations which provide loans, such as the Public Works Loans Board that gives loans to Local Authorities.

Any national borrowing incurs interest charges that compound over time. Thus an important NLF outgoing is the paying of interest on gilts and on

NS&I accounts. When the interest the NLF receives on its loans is less than the interest which it has to pay out (which is usually the case), proceeds from government bond issuance usually make up the difference.

4.2.3. *The Debt Management Account (DMA)*

The DMA, administered by the Debt Management Office, is the final stage in the chain that links government spending to government borrowing. It lies at the top of the Exchequer Pyramid shown in Figure 16 and is, in effect, the key gateway between the government and the wholesale financial markets (the 'money markets' in Figure 16). Established in 1998, its purpose is:

> *...to carry out the Government's debt management policy of minimising financing costs over the longer term, taking account of risk, and to manage the aggregate cash needs of the Exchequer in the most cost-effective way.*[146]

Just as with the Consolidated Fund and the NLF, the DMA is an account at the Bank of England, although unlike the other two it is run by an executive agency of HM Treasury (the Debt Management Office) rather than the Treasury itself.

The Debt Management Office transacts with the markets using various instruments. The main instruments are gilts[147] and Treasury bills (Box 3, Chapter 2),* which are sold into the market from the DMA. Finally the Debt Management Office can also borrow from the market through sale and repurchase agreements (repos), and lend to the market through reverse sale and repurchase agreements (reverse repos) (Figure 16).

The Debt Management Office sells new gilts in what is known as the primary market, via an auction mechanism.† In 2010 and 2011, they planned to sell a total of £148.1 billion of gilts. These would be sold almost exclusively to its 'primary dealers' – the gilt-edged market-makers (GEMMs; Box 10).[148] The money that is received for these gilts is transferred to the DMA, and from there it is sent to the NLF, then to the Consolidated Fund, before finally being spent into the economy.

---

* The main difference between Treasury bills and gilts is their term to maturity – Treasury bills have maturities of between 1 and 12 months, whereas gilts generally have maturities of between 3 and 50 years.

† Conventional gilts are sold by 'multiple price auctions' and indexed gilts sold in 'uniform price auctions'. However, the Debt Management Office can and does sell gilts using other methods. In 2010/ 2011 it also plans to sell £29.2 billion gilts by appointing private banks to sell the bonds on the DMOs behalf (known as 'syndication'), and £10 billion through 'mini tenders' which address emergency pockets of demand in various gilts. There are also many other types of auction which the Debt Management Office may use to sell or buy gilts, although none are planned for 2010/2011. HM Treasury, *Debt and Reserves Management Report 2010-2011*, p. 28. London: HM Treasury.

Box 10: Market-makers

A market-maker is a broker-dealer firm that accepts the risk of holding a certain number of shares of a particular security in order to facilitate trading in that security. Each market-maker competes for customer orders by displaying buy and sell quotations for a guaranteed number of shares. Once an order is received, the market-maker immediately sells from its own inventory or seeks an offsetting order. This process takes place in mere seconds. Market-makers profit from the difference between what they buy and sell their shares for.

In the UK, gilt-edged market makers (GEMMS) are licensed by the government to deal in gilts (government bonds). There are currently 20 GEMMS in the UK and they are mainly larger investment banks – see http://www.dmo.gov.uk/index.aspx?page=Gilts/Gemms_idb for a full list.

Market-makers play an important role in keeping the financial markets running efficiently because they are willing to quote both bid and offer prices for an asset.

Once a gilt has been sold to a GEMM on the primary market, it can be taken and resold on a secondary market. The secondary market is important because it makes a previously illiquid asset (a gilt with a fixed redemption date) liquid. Those who have bought gilts but wish to sell them before redemption can do so. This raises demand for bonds from the level they would have been at without a secondary market, and allows investors to hold liquid assets, whilst they still receive the benefits of having a fixed repayment date. Furthermore, the price of gilts in secondary markets is determined by genuine supply and demand rather than the primary market where GEMMS are required to both buy and sell gilts on demand at any time.[149] This price mechanism conveys important information to investors that will also affect the primary market.

As we have seen, government spending, via the Consolidated Fund, is usually financed by taxation and borrowing. In terms of intrabank payment, the process is no different from ordinary transfers, as described in Section 3.3. If a customer buys bonds or pays tax, the money moves from their commercial bank account to the government's bank account at the Bank of England via transfers of central bank reserves.

At the end of each working day, any public funds in the Exchequer Pyramid (Figure 16) at the Bank of England are 'swept up' to the NLF, which itself is swept into the DMA. The Debt Management Office has an agreement with the Bank of England to hold a certain cash balance every night to offset any late or unexpected outflows. If it exceeds the targeted balance, the Debt Management Office invests the surplus on the money markets until it is needed; if it is short of the target, it borrows the shortfall through the overnight or longer-term money markets. If public bodies do not minimise the balances in their own accounts with commercial banks and place funds in their Exchequer accounts, the amount of net government borrowing outstanding on any given day will be appreciably higher, adding to interest costs and making the fiscal position worse.[150]

In 2004, the Bank of England announced that it would stop providing retail banking services and focus on its core purpose of maintaining monetary and fiscal stability by the end of 2009. The Government Banking Service was launched in May 2008. It incorporates the Office of HM Paymaster General and is the new banking shared service provider for the public sector. Contracts with the RBS and Citibank have replaced the seven banking providers previously used by HM Revenue and Customs and National Savings and Investments. The banking services covered by the contracts include all transactions and account management functions, but the money itself remains with the Bank of England and therefore inside the Exchequer Pyramid (Figure 17). The new arrangements with the commercial banks also mean there is no need to re-tender for back-office services, with public bodies being able to interact directly with the banks on-line.[151]

4.3. The effect of government borrowing on the money supply: crowding out

Government borrowing can affect the price and quantity of money available to the private sector – a process known as **crowding out**. The textbook crowding-out argument states that when a government borrows from the market, it has in effect to persuade the private sector to give up resources so that it can use them. By adding its supply of government bonds, the government effectively borrows a limited amount of money that otherwise would have been used by the private sector, making money more scarce and thus driving up interest rates.

However, empirically, this crowding-out effect via higher interest rates has been difficult to establish.[152] A simpler, quantity-based form of crowding out has been empirically supported: When investors purchase newly issued government bonds with existing purchasing power, this money is withdrawn from the private sector and given to the government. Hence pure fiscal policy – that is, not connected to changes in monetary factors – is growth-neutral: it is a pure redistribution policy. While receivers of government funds will be better off, there are those who receive fewer government funds or pay higher taxes, and their financial condition has worsened by the same amount. Thus fiscal policy is a zero-sum game in terms of its implications for growth.

Box 11: Linking fiscal policy to increased credit creation

It is, however, possible to increase the impact of fiscal policy by linking it to credit creation. This can be done in a number of ways. The easiest would be for the central bank to purchase, indirectly, through the secondary market, the government bonds newly issued to fund fiscal expansion, while not counteracting these purchases through any of its other transactions.

An alternative that is easy to implement by the government when it cannot be sure of the long-term cooperation of the central bank, is to stop the issuance of government bonds and borrow instead directly from commercial banks in the form of long-term loan contracts. This has the advantage of increasing bank credit creation, as well as strengthening the banking system by improving the quality of its loan book.

In response to the UK banking crisis, the government chose to do the opposite: it borrowed money from the markets to finance a bailout of the banking system.* This was partially counteracted, however, by the central bank buying back government bonds through the programme of quantitative easing.

For nominal growth to take place, more transactions contributing to GDP must take place, and this means more money must have been used for such transactions. In our financial system, however, this is only possible if more commercial bank money (digital credit) has been created. Without credit creation (the creation of new purchasing power), the income pie is unchanged. Then any increase in government spending will merely increase the government's share of the pie – and hence must reduce the private sector's share of the same pie.[153]

So fiscal policy funded through bond issuance tends to 'crowd out' private sector consumption and investment, since often it is not connected to an increase in the money supply. Therefore, if there is no impact on the quantity of money, there will only be an expansionary impact on the economy if the government uses the money more productively than the original private sector holders would have done. This does not mean that it has no rightful place in government policy. However, users of fiscal policy should be under no illusions about its impact.

If government spending fully crowds out private sector investment, then the question becomes how the composition of investment varies between public and private sectors. While a discussion of the government's ability to spend money in a more economically productive manner than the private sector is beyond the scope of this book, a few points should be considered.

---

* For further detail on the cost to the UK taxpayer of supporting the banking sector see Prieg, L., Greenham, T. and Ryan-Collins, J. (2011). *Quid Pro Quo: Redressing the privileges of the banking industry.* London: **nef**.

First, private investors will put their money where they receive the highest returns. Thus any private individual is likely to invest at least part of their money abroad. While this may result in a higher private return than if they had invested locally, the entire social benefit of the investment will fall abroad.

Similarly, the government can also choose to invest in projects where the social return outweighs the private return, or in projects that have long term growth benefits, which otherwise would be underfunded. It should also be borne in mind that the UK government has a lower risk premium than any private borrower due to the lower chance of default, and can therefore borrow more cheaply than the private sector.

Finally, the private sector can and does borrow money for non-productivity-enhancing purposes, such as speculation, mortgage finance, and consumption. The government therefore can invest in a socially more beneficial way than the private sector. Although this is, of course, no guarantee that it will have the right information to invest productively, or even try to do so.

4.4. Government and central bank foreign reserves

Historically, the UK has held foreign currency reserves so it could intervene in order to regulate the exchange value of sterling. However, there have been no government interventions to influence the sterling exchange rates since 1992, when the UK exited the Exchange Rate Mechanism (ERM), although there have been two interventions since then to support foreign currencies. The first of these occurred in September 2000 when the UK government and the other G7 countries intervened in order to prevent any further depreciation in the value of the euro. The second occurred on 18 March 2011, when the UK government and the other G7 countries intervened in order to prevent any further appreciation of the yen following the earthquake that hit Japan on 11 March. Both interventions were performed by the Bank of England, via the EEA.[154]

Other than intervening to support a currency, foreign exchange reserves are now held primarily for three reasons.

1. As a precautionary measure – in case of any future changes to exchange rate policy or unexpected shocks.

2. To provide foreign currency services to government.

3. To buy, sell, and hold Special Drawing Rights (SDRs), as required by membership of the International Monetary Fund (IMF).[155]

Of course, foreign exchange reserves may also be held due to decisions made collectively by consumers and investors: If a country earns more on its exports than it imports, foreign exchange reserves will accumulate. Often, they are used by investors to fund overseas investments. However, this need not be the case. Norway, for instance, has found it impossible to maintain imports and capital outflows in line with foreign exchange accumulation due to oil exports. Consequently, foreign exchange reserves have accumulated. One issue with this is that foreign exchange earnings cannot be directly used for domestic spending – the money can only be spent abroad or on imports.

4.4.1. The Exchange Equalisation Account (EEA)

The government holds its foreign exchange reserves in the EEA and the NLF. The EEA reserves consist of gold, foreign currency assets, and SDRs (see Appendix 3 for a table of the current balances). The NLF reserves consist of the Reserve Tranche Position (RTP) at the IMF and bilateral loans to the IMF.[156] The EEA is funded by central government through the NLF, via a sterling account which the EEA maintains with the NLF. This allows the NLF to advance funds to the EEA, and for the EEA to repay funds to the NLF.[157]

Unlike the other main government accounts, the EEA is managed by the Bank of England, not the Treasury. Furthermore, other than the gold coin and bullion, the EEA's foreign reserves are not held at the Bank of England, rather, the EEA is composed of five accounts held at four banks – two in dollars (held at Federal Reserve Bank of New York and at JP Morgan Chase Bank); one in euro (held at Clearstream); and two in yen (held at Bank of Japan and JP Morgan Chase Bank).[158]

As well as managing the reserves by investing in foreign currency assets,[*] the Bank also acts as the Treasury's agent for foreign currency liability management, which includes issuing debt (originating from the NLF) denominated in foreign currency in order to finance some of the reserves.[159]

4.4.2. Bank of England foreign exchange reserves

The Bank of England maintains its own separate, smaller pool of foreign exchange reserves, which it may use to intervene in foreign exchange markets in support of its monetary policy objectives.[160] Since December 2006, the

---

[*] In the main these are bonds issued or guaranteed by the government of the USA, Euro area countries and Japan, gold, and SDRs, although other assets are also used. These include: securities issued by other national governments, supranational organisations and selected government and government-sponsored agencies; Pfandbriefe (a mostly triple-A-rated German bank bond); foreign currency spot, forward and swap transactions; interest rate and currency swaps; bond, interest rate and swap futures; sale and repurchase agreements; forward rate agreements; deposits with the Bank; deposits with, and certificates of deposits issued by, highly rated banks; and corporate commercial paper and bonds. HM Treasury. *Exchange Equalisation Account: Report and Accounts 2009-10.* London: HM Treasury, para 16.

Bank's reserves have been financed by issuing medium-term securities on an annual basis (March 2007, 2008, 2009, 2010). The most recent (2011) issue, is a $2 billion, three-year Eurobond, paying a coupon of 1.375 per cent, which matures on 7 March 2014. The Bank employs commercial banks as its agents to sell these bonds in the market.[161]

4.5. Foreign exchange, capital flows, and monetary policy: the 'impossibility trinity'

A foreign exchange market is simply a marketplace (physical or virtual) for buyers and sellers of different currencies and is essential to the modern globalised economy. Foreign exchange arises out of the need for people who are trading across borders to get hold of the local currency in order to pay local sellers.

While the goods produced in a country are priced in terms of that country's currency (one loaf of bread = £1.20), the currency of a country is priced in terms of other currencies (£1 = $1.63 = €1.13). The price of currencies is known as the **exchange rate**, and is quoted in pairs of currencies.

By 2010 the foreign exchange market had grown to be the largest and most liquid market in the world, with an average of $4 trillion of currency being exchanged (settled*) every day.[162] Banks located in the United Kingdom dominate the foreign exchange market, accounting for 37 per cent of all foreign exchange market turnover.[163] Of the currencies that are traded, the US dollar is the most prominent, accounting for 85 per cent of all transactions. The other key currencies are the euro (accounting for 37 per cent of all transactions), the Japanese yen (accounting for 17.2 per cent of all transactions) and the pound sterling (accounting for 14.9 per cent of all transactions).[164]

For most people, the only time they will ever need foreign exchange is when they are going on holiday. However, these transactions make up only a tiny proportion of all foreign exchange trades. The major private sector players in the foreign exchange markets are businesses and speculators.

---

* In the forex markets the term 'settlement' refers to the completion of the transaction and fulfilment of the contract – i.e. for a spot transaction settlement would occur when both currencies have been delivered (electronically) to the buyer and the seller's bank accounts, normally two days after the deal was done (spot rates).

We go in to some detail as to how the foreign exchange payment system works in Appendix 4. Here we provide a simple explanation of how foreign exchange effects commercial bank money and reserves.

Let's say that Jim has a US bank account, and wants the money transferred to a UK bank account. His US bank will have to do a 'spot trade' (see Appendix 4) with a UK bank exchanging dollars for pounds. For the sake of argument imagine its a huge amount of money and so the banks need to exchange central bank reserves so as not to be short. In the US the US bank will send $ reserves from its account at the Federal Reserve (the US central bank) to the UK bank's account at the Federal Reserve (both exchanges taking place in the US monetary system).

In the UK the UK bank will send £ reserves from its account at the BoE to the US bank's account at the BoE (all in the UK system). In terms of reserves the US bank has received pound reserves for dollar reserves, and the UK bank has in exchange received dollar reserves for pound reserves. Thus in both countries the level of reserves is the same.

Jim now has a bank account in the UK with pounds and in exchange his bank account in America has less dollars.

In reality, if both commercial banks have reserve accounts at both central banks it is likely that bar a huge sum of money being exchanged neither bank would need to adjust its reserves and, as with the UK interbank market, they would simply net out the change. The key point to note is foreign exchange transactions do not affect the level of reserves in aggregate in the banking system.

4.5.1. Exchange rate regimes

As discussed in Chapter 2, the UK has moved from having a gold-backed currency to a pegged exchange rate and finally to a free-floating exchange rate. In this section we briefly review these different models and their relation to monetary policy. More detail on foreign exchange is provided in Appendix 4.

When countries adhere to the gold standard, the exchange rate depends upon the amount of gold, silver, or copper contained in the coins of each country. A coin containing ten grams of gold would exchange for two coins containing five grams of gold, and so on. However, it is also possible to have a fixed exchange rate regime with a fiat currency. These can come in several forms, the most common of which is a pegged regime. Under a pegged regime, the government sets the price of the domestic currency in terms of a foreign currency. So for instance, in 1991 Argentina fixed its exchange rate against the dollar, so that one peso could be converted to one dollar on demand at the central bank.

Other types of pegged regimes include **crawling pegs** and **currency bands**. Under a crawling peg, the exchange rate is allowed to appreciate or depreciate slowly to allow for differing rates of inflation between the two countries. This stops goods in one country becoming relatively more expensive than in the other country, preserving the so-called real exchange rate (the exchange rate in terms of goods). Conversely, currency bands allow the exchange rate to float freely, although only within a narrow range. Perhaps the most prominent currency band in recent history was the European Monetary System, which between 1978 and 1998 determined the value of exchange rates in the European Union.

4.5.2. *Government intervention to manage exchange rates*

So how does a fixed exchange rate work in practice? The government or central bank cannot just announce the rate it wants and then expect it to magically occur. Instead, the central bank must stand ready to intervene in foreign exchange markets by buying and selling its own currency. For example, imagine you are the central bank of Argentina in 1991, and the exchange rate is fixed at one peso to one dollar. Due to a fantastic new investment opportunity in America, Argentineans start selling pesos and buying dollars, leading to downward pressure on the price of pesos in terms of dollars. Argentina's central bank steps in, selling dollars and buying pesos, and in doing so maintains the one-to-one exchange rate.[*]

In contrast to fixed exchange rate regimes, floating regimes can do away with any central bank involvement in the foreign exchange market, with market forces determining the exchange rate. Currently most of the world's major currencies operate on a floating exchange regime.[†] Under a floating regime, if Britons wish to invest in Europe they have to sell their pounds and buy euro, and all other things being equal, this pushes up the price of the euro in terms of pounds. This is known as an appreciation of the euro or, equivalently, as a depreciation of the pound.

---

[*] The process is actually far more complex than described here. Of particular importance is the fact that central bank reserves (in pesos) are transferred to the central bank, removing them from the system. Without any offsetting by the central bank the reduction in reserves can lead to an increase in the interbank rate. The reasons for the inability of the central bank to control its own monetary policy under a fixed exchange rate regime are discussed in the 'impossible trinity' section, 4.6.1.

[†] However, in certain extreme situations a central bank may intervene in order to stabilize exchange rates. For instance, on 18 March 2011, the UK government and the other G7 countries intervened in order to prevent any further appreciation of the yen, following the earthquake that hit Japan on the 11 March. Thus, these regimes are sometimes known as 'managed' or 'dirty' floats.

Figure 17: The impossibility trinity.

So why is the choice of exchange rate regime important? Obviously it will directly affect those who wish to buy or sell foreign currency. However, the choice of exchange regime will also affect the ability of the central bank to pursue autonomous monetary policy. If a country chooses to have a fixed exchange rate and free capital flows,* then monetary policy must be used to maintain the value of the currency. It is not possible to simultaneously maintain free capital flows, a fixed exchange rate, and an autonomous monetary policy. This is known as the **impossibility trinity** (Figure 17). Members of a currency union such as the euro zone are effectively operating a fixed exchange rate regime – so fixed in fact, that the currencies have been merged into a single currency. In a world of free capital flows, this is why countries such as Greece, Spain, Portugal, and Ireland are unable to pursue a sovereign monetary policy tailored to their individual economic circumstances.

To see why this is so, consider a country with a fixed exchange rate regime. If the central bank of this country tried to lower its interest rate in order to stimulate the domestic economy, then residents of the country may look to transfer their savings into foreign assets, to take advantage of the relatively higher interest rate abroad. In order to do so, they could begin to sell the domestic currency, likely leading to the price falling due to the sudden extra supply. However, the central bank is committed to maintaining the

---

* Couldn't a country just restrict capital flows? Yes, it could – as has successfully been done by Malaysia, after the outbreak of the Asian crisis (initially opposed, but today lauded by the IMF for this policy), and for many decades, the People's Republic of China. The implementation may not be perfect, due to large firms attempting to disguise capital flows as current account transactions, etc.

exchange rate. In order to stop the currency depreciating, it has to sell its foreign exchange for domestic currency. However, people may continue to shift into foreign assets for as long as there is a difference between the interest rates. So unless the central bank increases the interest rate, the selling of the domestic currency may continue until the Bank's foreign exchange reserves are exhausted. At this point the central bank will no longer be able to support the currency – leading to its devaluation. Of course, this will break the central bank's commitment to the fixed exchange rate. Thus, in a world of free capital flows, fixing the exchange rate requires giving up monetary policy autonomy, and vice versa. An example of this was the UK's response to Black Wednesday – 16 September 1992, when the UK Conservative government was forced to withdraw the pound from the ERM due to pressure by currency speculators. The Bank of England raised interest rates massively in order to stem capital outflows and maintain the exchange rate – ultimately without success as investors did not believe that the interest rate increases were credible.

4.6. Summary

This section has demonstrated how the UK government is severely constrained in its ability to create new money, in contrast to the commercial banking sector. This is mainly due to EU legislation which removed the power of direct credit creation from governments by banning the monetisation of government debt by national central banks. Governments can, of course, raise funds through the issuance of bonds as they always have done but because these cannot be monetised before they reach the secondary market, the effect in terms of fiscal policy would appear to be neutral – funds are simply moved from one part of the economy to another. The financial crisis of 2007/2008 and current sovereign debt crisis are placing significant strains on these arrangements, with the ECB being forced to buy significant government debt in attempt to prevent sovereign defaults. Further constraints to monetary policy and autonomy come through the choice of exchange rate regime.

Chapter 5 examines how, within the international constraints outlined, the UK government attempts to manage money creation through the regulation of commercial banks.

5. Managing money creation: Regulating banks

There can be no doubt that besides the regular types of the circulating medium, such as coin, notes and bank deposits, which are generally recognised to be money or currency, and the quantity of which is regulated by some central authority or can at least be imagined to be so regulated, there exist still other forms of media of exchange which occasionally or permanently do the service of money ... [I]t is clear that, other things equal, any increase or decrease of these money substitutes will have exactly the same effects as an increase or decrease of the quantity of money proper, and should therefore, for the purposes of theoretical analysis, be counted as money."

Friedrich Hayek, 1931[165]

We have now completed our review of historical developments and the present-day workings of the modern UK monetary system. We have seen that the popular and textbook conceptions of banking outlined in Chapter 1 are out-dated and misleading. Commercial banks are the main creators of credit and thus of money in the UK economy.

In this chapter, we examine the external constraints on the creation of new commercial bank money. In particular, we examine regulations imposed on banks' liquidity (the amount of highly liquid assets they hold) and their provision against insolvency (the amount of capital they hold). We shall see that both liquidity and capital ratios fell relentlessly in the period from 1970 to the start of the financial crisis of 2007–2008. There are a number of reasons for this. In Chapters 2 and 3 we described the deregulation, digitisation, and the emergence of the modern payment system, and also theoretical misconceptions about the nature of credit markets. We now also consider briefly the emergence of the 'shadow banking' system, before analysing the limits of liquidity and capital constraints.

5.1. Securitisation, shadow banking, and the financial crisis

To circumvent the Basel regulations on capital adequacy, banks discovered a new method to preserve their capital adequacy and maintain liquidity whilst continuing to expand credit creation. They could 'securitise' their loans. Securitisation is the process of selling on a loan, or a package of loans, and passing the risk and reward onto someone else in exchange for cash. By taking loans off the bank's balance sheet, it can create capacity for new lending while staying with the required capital ratios.

Depending on the quality, quantities, and streams of interest accruing to them, the bank can make a judgment as to whether it will be profitable to hold a loan or set of loans or to sell them. Because banks 'originate' the loans in the first place – and larger investment banks in particular have huge teams of analysts spread across the world looking at the latest developments in financial markets – they are quite often in a better position to judge the quality of a loan or set of loans than the buyer of the securitised loans. There is an asymmetry of information. Banks which merely originate loans which they intend to sell on to others have less of an incentive to be careful in their analysis of credit risk and the sustainability of these loans. As a result, the banks can play the market to ensure capital adequacy levels are kept up and they expand their lending, while systemic risk in the economy increases. This is another example of the problem that arises when banks are given the public privilege of creating new money, but have not been given any guidance as to how this should be done in order to contribute to general prosperity and stability.

The financial crisis has been widely attributed to the 'originate and distribute' model of banking that investment banks began engaging in on a large scale from the early 2000s. In particular, there was rapid growth in the market for residential mortgage-backed securities (RMBSs). This involved the creation of packages of different mortgage loans of different levels of riskiness which were securitised and sold on to investors – often long-term investors such as insurance companies and pension funds and even local and regional authorities. However, many of these securities were backed by American 'sub-prime' mortgages, that is, loans to high-risk borrowers. These began to default when house prices in the USA collapsed in 2006.

Because no one knew where exactly in these complex securities particular sub-prime mortgages actually were held or how widely they had been spread, banks suddenly became very risk-averse about the true value not only of other banks' balance sheets but also of their own. They suddenly became reluctant to lend to each other in the interbank market, which created severe balance sheet problems for all banks.

Box 12: The 'shadow banking' system

The 'shadow banking system' is a loose term used to cover the proliferation of financial activities undertaken by banks off their balance sheets, largely beyond the reach of regulation. No solid definition yet exists, but it conventionally includes non-depository money market funds, the use of securitisation and credit derivatives by many institutions, and private repo transactions.[166]

What all these have in common, aside from their extraordinary expansion over the last decade, is the creation of forms of credit that have no relationship to traditional banking. As discussed previously, it is quite possible for banks to create money and credit out of nothing. The shadow banking system hugely extends that principle, in different ways. For example, securitised collateral, typically in the form of loans repackaged to receive AAA grade ratings, could be used in a repo transaction. The asset would be sold to another institution, with an agreement to buy back at a later date, at a higher price. The seller would, in effect, be 'borrowing' the money, with the difference in price being equivalent to the interest rate. Repo transactions have therefore been called another type of privately created money,[167] which form a crucial part of the shadow banking system.

By its nature, estimating the size of the shadow system can be difficult,[168] although it is likely now to be somewhat larger than conventional banking. As of early 2007, Timothy Geithner, then President of the Federal Reserve Bank of New York (an institution privately owned by the member banks, and the key central bank in the Federal Reserve System in the US, as it is the main locus of central bank OMOs), suggested the US shadow banking system had assets under management to the value of $10.5 trillion, or about $500 billion larger than the US deposit banking system at the time.[169]

This was close to the peak of the market; the crash of 2007/2008 has been described as a 'run' on the shadow banking system, in which confidence in the complex structures of unregulated credit creation evaporated, leaving the US banking system 'effectively insolvent for the first time since the Great Depression' as the crisis spread into conventional banking.[170] Colossal injections of government funds in those countries worst affected by the crash have stabilised and restored confidence to the system, promoting a further boom in its activities (while sharply raising national debt, keeping such operations on the central bank balance sheet would not have created any liabilities for tax-payers), but the underlying weaknesses of an unregulated, off-balance-sheet credit system have not been addressed. Since the crash, Basel III and other efforts at regulatory reform have instead focused very heavily on the capital and liquidity provisions of commercial banks.

5.2. Protecting against insolvency: capital adequacy rules

We discussed in Chapter 3 the importance of bank solvency and the importance of banks having sufficient capital to cover defaults on their loans. The theory goes that by making banks hold a certain amount of capital, they should be able to survive if a significant number of their assets become non-performing, for instance, due to default on loans. If most banks in an economy have this buffer, then it is hoped that banks will retain enough confidence in other banks to continue lending reserves on the interbank market and that individuals will not rush to withdraw their deposits. Solvent banks should therefore be less likely to suffer a liquidity crisis.

The Basel Committee on Banking Supervision (BCBS) has formulated recommendations concerning required bank capital. The Committe is a private body of central banks and regulators linked to the Bank for International Settlement (BIS).[*] Commonly referred to as the Basel Accord, the BCBS rules, while formally non-binding on any national regulator, are in practice adopted by national or European (Brussels) financial regulatory authorities and thus have become binding on banks.[†] First introduced in 1988, their goal is not to ensure a particular allocation of credit or to help authorities in steering the quantity of credit created. They are only said to be helpful in limiting credit creation indirectly and in assuring solvency of banks. The recent banking crisis, however, has shown that they do not fulfil these goals. Whether the latest round of revised Basel rules (known as Basel III) is an improvement remains to be seen.

According to the rules, banks must set aside a certain amount of capital every time they make a loan. Capital can be derived from retained profits or money raised from investors (including the owners of the bank, the shareholders) as we discussed in Chapter 3. This is also called the **own capital** or **own funds** of the bank. Just like deposits or credits, own funds are an accounting entry, but in contrast to deposits they cannot be withdrawn. Instead, they are used when the bank suffers losses, such as when a borrower defaults on a loan. In that case, the same amount would be reduced from loans on the asset side and from the own capital on the liability side. Since capital usually is less than a tenth of assets (which include bank loans, sovereign debt, and derivatives such as Exchange Traded Funds[‡] and Collateralised Debt Obligations[§]) a 10 per cent default of loans would wipe out all capital and render the bank insolvent. A smaller loss would leave it in breach of capital adequacy rules, requiring it to shrink its lending or raise more capital. When there is too large a proportion of bad assets, own capital – that is, the net worth of the bank – can become negative.

Being able to use retained earnings as capital means that every time a bank makes a profit, it can set some aside as capital, which enables further lending, which leads to further profits, which further increases capital. Therefore, under

---

[*]   The BIS itself developed out of the Reparations Committee established under the leadership of JP Morgan after WWI.

[†]   For a detailed history of the Basel Rules pre-Basel II, see Goodhart, C. (2011). *The Basel Committee on Banking Supervision: A History of the Early Years, 1974-1997* [Hardcover], Cambridge University Press: Cambridge.

[‡]   Exchange traded funds allow investors to track the prices of a bundle of different assets.

[§]   Collateralised Debt Obligations combine parts of a large member of loans into a new 'composite' asset.

a stable capital ratio, a bank's balance sheets can expand at the same rate of increase as its retained profits.

In the current system of regulation, loans are given a risk weighting depending on how risky the regulators perceive the loan to be. Business loans are given a 100 per cent risk weighting, meaning that for regulatory purposes, the level of capital currently required must be 8 per cent of the value of the loan. Under Basel II rules, large banks can further refine the regulators risk weighting to suit their own particular risk profiles according to their own internal assessments of risk. The level of capital required is currently being discussed by domestic and international regulators and is set to go up. In the UK, following the Independent Commission on Banking's final report published in September 2011, it is expected to be raised to 10 per cent for the retail banking subsidiaries of large banking groups.

So, if a business borrows £1,000, £80 of capital must be kept aside for a capital requirement of 8 per cent, as the loan is risk weighted at 100 per cent. Mortgages are given a lower risk weighting, as the house can be sold to someone else if the homeowner cannot pay. Mortgages are currently weighted at 35 per cent. This means that a £1,000 mortgage would only require £28 of capital (£1,000 x 35 per cent risk weighting x 8 per cent capital ratio), which is the same level of capital that a £350 business loan would require. From this it follows that unless a business loan makes three times as much profit as a mortgage, the bank will prefer to extend mortgages.

5.2.1. Why capital adequacy requirements do not limit credit creation

Because retained profits can count as capital, the more profitable a bank is, the more loans it can make. And, as we discussed, bank loans are rather special since they do not actually cost the bank anything to create, but the bank can charge very profitable rates of interest on them.

It should be clear by now that increasing capital adequacy ratios will not necessarily stop an increase in bank credit creation when the times are good, for three main reasons:

1. An economic boom, and particularly rising asset/collateral values, will encourage each individual bank to lower its estimates of risk, and hence of the level of capital it requires.

2. A more favourable view of economic prospects will also encourage the bank to make more loans, generating additional profits which increase its capital and allow it to make more loans.

3. In boom times, when regulators may in the future impose higher capital
   adequacy requirements as a counter-cyclical 'macro-prudential' policy,
   banks will find it easier to raise more capital, as the money to purchase it
   is ultimately created by the banking system, and an increasing amount is
   created during boom times (hence the boom in the first place).

Furthermore, different dynamics come into play when we distinguish between an
individual bank, and the banking system as a whole. As we argued in Section 3.3,
if the banks expand their balance sheets in step, there is little to restrain them. If
only one bank continues to lend, it will find that it bumps up against its capital
adequacy and liquidity limits, but if all banks are lending and creating new
deposits, provided they remain willing to lend to one another, the banking system
in aggregate will generate enough additional capital and liquidity.

In other words, the Basel capital adequacy arrangements reinforce the pro-
cyclicality of the banking system. At best, the delay before growth in earnings
from new lending shows up as capital will act as a 'drag' on balance sheet
growth. And the same applies the other way round. If banks become concerned
about the economy and their balance sheets, they will be less keen to make
loans that might default and reduce their capital adequacy.

More fundamentally, analysis of capital adequacy rules usually neglects the
crucial fact that banks are the creators of the money supply. Thus requiring
banks to raise more capital in the boom times won't stop the boom. The boom
is caused by increased bank credit, and some of the expansion in the money
supply can be tapped by banks to fund higher capital ratios.[171,172]

5.2.2. Leverage Ratios: a variant of capital adequacy rules

In 2009, the G-20 Committee of Finance Ministers and central bank governors
and the Financial Stability Board, an international committee of central bank
regulators and national finance ministries, have proposed to introduce a
leverage ratio to supplement the risk-based regulatory capital adequacy ratio.

There are two common definitions of a leverage ratio. Firstly, the Canadian
definition which is total assets to total capital including equity and
subordinated debt. This is to say that the leverage ratio is simply the inverse of
Basel capital adequacy requirements but without the risk-weighting procedures.
The US and European definition has been even more similar to the Basel
capital adequacy, as it defines the leverage ratio as equity capital as a proportion
of adjusted assets.

The discussion of leverage ratios is thus similar to a discussion of capital adequacy rules. Stricter capital adequacy rules mean to require banks to hold more capital, which is to say that the banks will have lower leverage. As such, this proposal is not a new suggestion, but in the long Basel tradition of the 1980s which, critics argue, has allowed Japanese, Asian and North Atlantic banking crises, among others.

Leverage ratios are therefore also an indirect and inadequate way of trying to control bank credit. Historically the only, and almost always effective method of controlling bank credit has been via direct credit controls. These work as follows: the central bank tells the banks that they extend credit for transactions that are not part of GDP (i.e. asset/financial transactions, including lending to hedge funds, etc.) by a certain absolute amount, expressed as a fraction of GDP (say 5 per cent). Or even stricter, they forbid such credit entirely. Banks would then have to focus on creating credit for transactions that are part of GDP. Among those, there should be further curbs on consumer loans, and either no ceiling or very high loan growth quotas for credit for investment in the production of goods and services and productivity enhancements, which are non-inflationary and growth-enhancing.

 Unlike direct control of credit, the leverage ratio (or capital adequacy) may not achieve the goal of avoiding asset bubbles or may not enable the authorities to achieve the desired amount of credit creation. Indeed, leverage can give a misleading picture of both the state of the banking system and that of the economy.

The leverage ratio has actually been imposed in the US for many years, but it failed to prevent the sub-prime crisis. The reason is that leverage ratio can fall while bank credit creation in total, as well as credit creation for financial transactions (not contributing to GDP) rises unabated. This is what happened in the US, according to a World Bank report on this topic.[*]

---

[*] The World Bank wrote in 2009 on the proposal to introduce a leverage ratio: 'One argument against the leverage ratio has been that the United States, despite having a leverage ratio in place, was at the epicenter of the global financial crisis. Why did the U.S. leverage ratio fail to provide the right warning signs? To answer this question, a good starting point is to analyze the evolution of leverage in the years running up to the financial crisis. Over the past decades financial innovation has fundamentally changed the structure of the financial system. ... Banks funded a growing amount of long-term assets with short-term liabilities in wholesale markets through the use of off-balance-sheet vehicles, exposing themselves to credit and liquidity risk by providing facilities to these vehicles. Moreover, they also held structured credit instruments on their own balance sheet, exposing themselves to embedded leverage and increasing their asset-liability mismatch and their funding liquidity risk. For major European and U.S. investment banks, balance sheet leverage multiples (measured as total assets divided by equity) increased during the four years preceding the global financial crisis (Figure 2). For Japanese and U.S. commercial banks, by contrast, aggregate balance sheet leverage did not increase over this period, and in some instances it even fell.' Retrieved from http://www.worldbank.org/financialcrisis/pdf/levrage-ratio-web.pdf

Figure 18: Bank of England balance sheet as a % of GDP.[173]

(a) Famine / End of railroad boom (1847)
(b) Overextension of credit from 1855–1866
(c) Failure to Overend Gurney (1866)
(d) Failure of City of Glasgow Bank (1878)

(e) Support for Barings (1890)
(f) WW1 (1914)
(g) Currency and Bank Note Act (1928)
(h) World War II (1941)

(i) Secondary Banking Crisis (1973)
(j) Small Banks Crisis (1991)
(k) Current Crisis (2007)

5.3. Regulating liquidity

If capital adequacy rules only weakly constrain credit creation can liquidity rules do any better?

We saw in Chapter 3 that there is a relationship between a bank's reserves with the Bank of England and the amount banks can lend. But it is not a relationship that fits with the 'banks as intermediaries' conception of banking that still dominates the public mind or the 'money multiplier' model of economics and finance textbooks. Banks don't intermediate the deposits they receive. Banks create brand new money whenever they want by extending credit or buying assets. As discussed in Section 3.5, the size of their reserves is mainly determined by banks' own estimates of what is needed to cover their everyday payment requirements, in consultation with the Bank of England.

Banks have not always made good decisions with regard to their liquidity and have regularly required the central bank to step in and provide injections of liquidity in order to prevent the collapse of the system. Figure 18 illustrates this, showing changes in the Bank of England's balance sheet as a percentage of GDP.

In the mid-nineteenth century, UK banks held on average 60 per cent of liquid assets as a proportion of total deposits, a ratio partly explained by the frequency of liquidity crises around that time.[174] Banks halved this ratio following the 1866 Overend and Gurney crisis when the Bank of England accepted a role as 'lender of last resort', committing to supply sufficient reserves to prevent future liquidity crises.

5.3.1. Compulsory reserve ratios

The first agreement on liquidity between the Bank of England and commercial banks occurred in 1947, when the privately owned Bank of England was nationalised. It involved a requirement to hold a minimum ratio of highly liquid assets (reserves, cash or Treasury bills) to deposits of 32 per cent (lowered to 27 per cent 16 years later). The regime prevailed until 1971, when the Competition and Credit Control policy regime (CCC) introduced a minimum reserve ratio of 12.5 per cent. As we saw in Chapter 3, CCC led to a massive decline in liquidity reserve ratios (Figure 7, Chapter 3).

After twice lowering the minimum requirement, the Bank of England finally abolished the compulsory reserve ratio regime with the cash ratio deposit regime in 1981, which did not directly require a minimum level of liquid assets.

5.3.2. Sterling stock liquidity regime (SLR)

The SLR, introduced in 1996, focused on holding sufficient liquidity to meet a particularly severe liquidity stress. It was calibrated to ensure that a bank had enough highly liquid assets to meet its outflows for the first week of a liquidity crisis without recourse to the market for renewed wholesale funding, in order to allow the authorities time to explore options for an orderly resolution. In the words of Nigel Jenkinson, responsible for financial stability at the Bank of England in 2008, the SLR was:

> *...designed as one component of a wider crisis management regime, and not as a means for a bank to manage its precautionary buffer for addressing liquidity strain on a going concern basis.*[175]

From 2006 up to 2009, the UK operated a 'corridor' system in which banks set their own reserve targets every month.[176,*] Reserve balances that on average over the month fell within a relatively narrow range around those targets were remunerated at Bank Rate. Outside this range, surplus reserves, which had been moved to the deposit facility, were remunerated at the lower deposit rate.

---

* For a full explanation of the changes in the Bank of England's interest rate regime, see Appendix 1.

In contrast, banks with insufficient reserves had to borrow those reserves at the higher lending rate.

The system worked for a short period with the money market rates staying relatively close to the Bank of England's rate, but from the summer of 2007, the financial crisis began and interbank market interest rates moved significantly above the Bank of England's rate. The Bank responded by making extra loans available since some banks were hoarding reserves and so the interbank market was not working efficiently. In addition, the Monetary Policy Commission (MPC) started rapidly cutting the Bank Rate, but whilst overnight interbank rates remained close to the policy rate, longer term interbank rates (for three-month loans, for instance) continued to be inflated.

The system of voluntary reserves was suspended in March 2009 following the decision of the Bank to embark on the purchase of financial assets funded through the creation of central bank money, more popularly known as quantitative easing.[177,178] The Bank ended up creating £200 billion worth of central bank reserves by buying government securities owned by the banks. The corridor system has now been replaced by a 'floor' system with the level of reserves initially being increased in line with asset purchases and all reserves remunerated at Bank Rate.

In December 2009, the Financial Services Authority (FSA) announced a new liquidity regime. Under this, each bank would have to hold a buffer of central bank reserves or gilts. Banks would be required to hold an amount determined by various 'stress tests', including an inability to access wholesale funding or rollover loans over a two-week period, and a 'sizeable retail outflow' (i.e. unusually large levels of withdrawals by bank customers).[179] At the time of the announcement, the FSA said it would wait until the recession was over and banks' balance sheets had improved before imposing the rules, and, as yet, agreements on this have not been put in place for individual banks. Recent reports suggest that a significant 'funding gap' still exists between banks' current holdings of highly liquid assets and the new requirements, suggesting it may be some time before the regulations come in to force.[180]

This is not the case in many other countries. In the United States, for example, there is still a 10 per cent liquidity reserve ratio on liabilities above $58.8 million.[181] In China, the government actively changes its liquidity reserve ratio to fight inflation; at the time of writing it stood at 20.5 per cent.*

---

* See footnote on page 20 for further details.

At the international level, there is a proposal to tighten liquidity regulations by insisting that all banks hold enough easy-to-sell assets to withstand a 30-day run on their funding, similar to the crisis that engulfed Lehman Brothers in 2008 and due to come in to force in 2015. At the time of writing, however, this 'liquidity coverage ratio' appeared likely to be softened by the Basel Committee on Banking Supervision as very few banks in Europe are near reaching these kind of liquidity levels given their exposure to the European sovereign debt crisis.[182]

5.4. The financial crisis as a solvency and liquidity crisis

The financial crisis revealed both the fragility of depending too much on the interbank lending market for liquidity and, hence, the weakness of the Bank's dependence on attempting to influence commercial bank money creation indirectly through changes to Bank of England rate and open market operations, as described in Chapter 3.

The credit creation process requires banks to utilise the interbank market to shift excess central bank money and/or bank money to those banks in need of it. This only works if banks can assume their solvency is largely unquestioned.

Bank solvency did begin to be questioned, however, in 2007. Problems in the US housing market and in particular doubts about the quality of sub-prime loans led to concerns spreading throughout the global banking system wherever these assets had been repackaged, securitised, and sold on. Rumours spread, and banks that are more dependent on such wholesale funding became the target of short sellers, while depositors increasingly shifted their funds away from them. By trading with a bank suspected of being insolvent, other banks would endanger their own solvency.

Very rapidly, banks lost confidence in each other's solvency. Banks also showed a reluctance to borrow reserves directly from the Bank of England using standing facilities, which prompted the creation of the Discount Window Facility (Section 3.7.3). The explanation for this also lies with confidence: it appears banks feared the reputational damage caused by borrowing from the standing facility was too great.

As a consequence, the interbank market virtually froze, and the interbank interest rate in London shot far above the Bank Rate. The central bank was no longer able to exert influence over the interbank rate. As we have seen, banks cover most of their borrowing needs in the interbank market. So this sudden rise in the market rate of interest and credit rationing between banks caused a liquidity crisis that threatened the payment system and the stability of the banking system in general.

When queues formed outside Northern Rock, the Bank of England was forced to step in, buying increasing amounts of assets from the banks in exchange for Bank of England reserves and cash that would enable them to make payments and rebuild their capital. Only by flooding banks and the interbank market with central bank reserves on a massive scale was the Bank able to avert financial collapse.

5.5. Endogenous versus exogenous money

We have seen then that the central bank cannot control bank money creation through adjusting the amount of central bank reserves banks must hold, as is implied in the multiplier model discussed in Chapter 1. It would be the case if people used cash for all their transactions, since banks are not permitted to create new banknotes. But as we have seen, people use their demand deposits for the great majority of payments and banks, through liability management, can always obtain the funds they need, provided the interbank markets are functioning smoothly, to settle their accounts.

In reality, rather than the Bank of England determining how much credit banks can issue, one could argue that it is the banks that determine how much central bank reserves and cash the Bank of England must lend to them (Section 3.3). The tail wags the dog. This follows from the Bank's acceptance of its position as lender of last resort (although it has not fully played this in the recent bank rescues, such as Northern Rock and RBS, since it passed on the bill for initial central bank money injections to the government and hence the tax-payers). When a commercial bank requests additional central bank reserves or cash, the Bank of England is not in position to refuse. If it did, the payment system described above would rapidly collapse.[183]

In academic terminology, this process is often described as **endogenous money creation**. Endogenous, loosely used in this context, means that the process is intrinsic to the workings of the economy.[184] Because cash and central bank reserves must be created on demand by the central bank whenever commercial banks request it, there is no obvious limit to the amount of this 'high-powered' money that the central bank must create. In this way, the money supply could be viewed as demand driven. This contrasts with the notion of exogenous money, whereby the money supply can be determined externally to the workings of the economy – for example, by the central bank adjusting its reserve ratio or interest rate. This latter approach, widely associated with monetarism and Milton Friedman,[185] was popular as a policy framework in the 1980s but has fallen out of favour.

However, there are inconsistencies when attempting to describe the money creation process as purely endogenous. Considering central bank money, while the central bank is likely to be forced to inject whatever reserves are needed to prevent banking activity from triggering monthly liquidity crises and interest rate volatility, this does not mean that the central bank is never in control of the money supply. The Bank of Japan, for instance, has been a strong supporter of the endogenous money approach, and it has argued for much of the past 20 years that it could not stimulate the economy, since money is demand-driven, and allegedly there simply has been very little demand for money in Japan. This argument is counter-intuitive, since SMEs have demanded credit consistently (and not received it), and record amounts of money were demanded by the Japanese government to fund fiscal expenditure.

The argument is also untrue since there is nothing that would have stopped the Bank of Japan injecting more money into the economy than required by the reserve needs of banks: it could simply purchase assets and thus bring new money into circulation. For instance, early on, the proposal was made that the Bank of Japan should boost the economy by increasing the money supply, and simultaneously boosting the property market (where values had fallen by about 80 per cent), and strengthening the banking sector, while increasing the quality of life in the large cities: Tokyo, for instance, is a major city with one of the lowest ratios of park acreage per capita. So the Bank of Japan could simply purchase, at attractive prices, unused or empty real estate and create public parks.[186,187] This would inject new purchasing power, support the property market and thus, by boosting collateral values, also help the banking system. In fact, the Japanese central bank has purchased properties in the past (albeit exclusively for the use of its own staff, such as beach resorts, golf courses, restaurants, and clubs in central Tokyo, etc.). Unfortunately, the central bank managed to hide behind the endogenous money argument, so that Japan's recession has now entered its third decade.

The second pillar of the endogenous money argument is that banks' credit creation always responds to the demand for bank loans. Anyone whose loan application has been turned down knows for sure that this is evidently not the case – banks ration credit, as will be discussed in Section 5.6. Consequently, credit creation is not purely endogenous to the economy, but it can be said that the central bank and the commercial banking sector together can determine credit creation exogenously and hence shape economic activity.

5.6. Credit rationing

The concept of credit rationing provides another explanation of why adjustments to the interest rate are likely to be a weak tool in controlling credit creation. We discussed in Chapter 2 why the idea of markets automatically clearing makes little sense as a description of reality. Without perfect information, there is nothing to ensure that demand will equal supply and that transaction prices are equilibrium prices. In a world such as ours, with imperfect information, markets do not automatically clear – so we are in a state of disequilibrium.[*] This means that markets are rationed and outcomes are determined by quantities, not prices.[188,189,190,191]

The outcome of these markets follows the short-side principle: whichever of demand or supply is smaller, that quantity will be transacted.[192] If I am a supplier of apples but only have ten apples, then I will only trade with you a maximum ten apples even if you want one hundred – and I may choose to sell you fewer. On the other hand, if you want just one apple I will be forced to sell you just one apple. Whoever is on the 'short side' has a major advantage, namely market power. This is perhaps most obviously felt when you are applying for a job. Could the job market for television news readers, for instance, ever be thought of as being in equilibrium? Since many people can read, while the pay and perks are attractive, there are likely to be more applicants than jobs.

The ubiquity of rationing also becomes obvious when we are trying to obtain tickets for the theatre, or, indeed, the Olympic Games. If, in aggregate, the amount supplied in a market is smaller than the amount demanded, the supply side is the short side and has market power. It could push up the price of the apples or gain other advantages and benefits and the buyers would have to put up with it. (The latter is again often felt in the labour market, or in the allocation of orders to contractors, where the decision-makers often demand – and obtain – what could be described as 'non-market' benefits or 'rents'; just think of the market for starlets in Hollywood productions and their reports on what they had to do to get the jobs.)

Is the credit market also rationed? This would not seem to fit with the idea of endogenous money we discussed earlier, which implies that, at the right level of interest, whatever money is demanded will be automatically supplied by the banks (and in turn reserves and cash by the Bank of England) and the credit market will 'clear'.

---

[*] See Goodhart, C. (1989). *Money, Information and Uncertainty*, Chapter VII: *Credit Rationing* for a good summary of theoretical and empirical debates on credit rationing.

But let's use some common sense. Money and credit are different from apples and, indeed, every other kind of commodity (in fact, as we have seen, money is not a commodity at all). Suppose you would like to have more pairs of shoes. But eventually, you will simply run out of space for shoes even if you are a princess living in a castle – you will want things other than shoes to be taking up your castle space. Economists call this declining marginal utility; each additional pair of shoes adds less utility than the last. However, having more money does not affect what other things you can or cannot have. It just means you can have more of anything. The demand for credit (and hence money) appears far less subject to diminishing marginal utility.[193]

Under the endogenous money theory, it is assumed that banks make loans, and credit 'clears' at a given interest rate. A riskier loan will incur a higher rate of interest. But if the dvemand for credit is always very high (or even infinite), the theoretical market-clearing interest rate would be so high as to leave them with only risky projects, while sensible projects could not generate sufficient returns to service the loans.[194] It is more important for a bank to avoid defaults on its loans than it is to earn a higher rate of interest. Higher rates may bring an extra few percentage points return, but a default could lead to a 100 per cent loss. As a result, and as economist Joseph Stiglitz showed in 1981, banks prefer to ration and allocate credit – even in the best of times.[195] Paul Tucker, Deputy Governor of the Bank of England, appears to agree:

> … *[households and companies]* … *are rationed in their access to credit, given that borrowers know a great deal more about their conditions and prospects than do risk-averse lenders, and that lenders face obstacles in ensuring that borrowers honour their contracts.*[196]

An interesting example of how credit rationing affects the macro-economy arises when comparing banks' incentives for mortgage lending vis à vis lending to small business. The owners of a small business may have limited liability. This means that if they take out a loan but the business fails, they will not be held personally liable in excess of their stake in the company. There are 'asymmetric' incentives between the business owner and the bank. The risk for the business owner of taking the loan is much smaller than for the bank.[197] In practice, banks often attempt to circumvent limited liability by seeking collateral from the directors or shareholders of the business, usually by taking a charge on their house. Thus, business loans may not even be granted to applicants who cannot provide such personal guarantees. Figure 19 suggests that banks in the UK have been moving increasingly in this direction in their lending activity – as can be seen in the huge growth in secured loans to individuals compared with lending to the productive sector.

Figure 19: Net lending by UK banks by sector, 1997-2010, sterling millions (Source: Bank of England Statistics- Interactive database)*

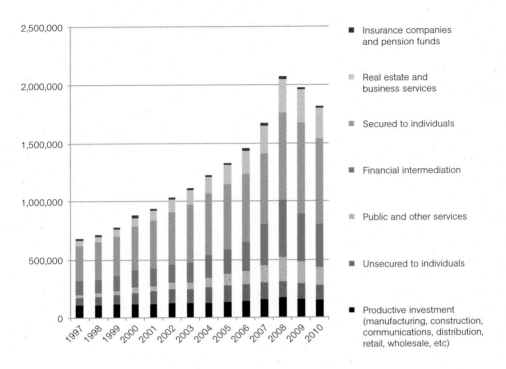

In contrast, if a bank issues a mortgage, it knows that if the borrower defaults, it will be able to repossess their house. The bank has access to the collateral. In the real world of imperfect information and hence lack of market clearing and credit rationing, a large bank that is focused on reliable and high profits will usually prefer to loan against collateral than against future cash flows. This discriminates against business investment because even in cases where the bank obtains collateral from the businesses owners or managers, the loan repayments will be made from the future cash flows that arise from the investment being funded by the loan. This requires careful scrutiny of the business case, and, crucially, good judgement from an experienced professional. Some form of market intervention will be required to change these incentives.

As economists Blanchard and Fischer point out, if credit rationing exists...

> *...it is possible that the interest rate is not a reliable indicator of the impact of financial variables on aggregate demand. It is quite likely in this case that variables measuring quantities, such as the amount of credit, have to be looked at in appraising monetary and financial policy.*[198]

Figure 20: Lending to small and medium-sized enterprises.

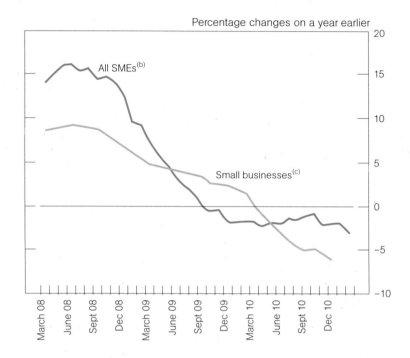

Sources: BBA, BIS and Bank calculations.

(a) Non seasonally adjusted

(b) Source: monthly BIS survey. Lending by four UK lenders to enterprises with annual bank account debit turnover less than £25 million. Data cover lending in both sterling and foreign currency, expressed in sterling terms.

(c) Source: BBA. Lending by seven UK lenders to commercial businesses with an annual bank account debit turnover of up to £1 million. Sterling only. Available at www.bba.org.uk/statistics/amll-business-support-december-2010/small-business/.

Empirical work on the Japanese economy, where interest rates were kept at very low levels throughout the 1990s in an effort to encourage lending and growth but banks continued to heavily ration credit, supports this thesis[199,200] – as indeed, does the current situation in the UK, where the Bank Rate has been kept at a record low level of 0.5 per cent since early 2009. Yet, net bank lending in particular to small businesses has continued to decline, becoming negative in September 2009 (Figure 20).[201] This is so despite the interbank rate also eventually returning to a level close to the Bank Rate.

Credit rationing by the banking system in aggregate will also lead to rationing in other markets.[202] If the credit being lent to small businesses is reduced, this will lead the businesses themselves to reduce their investment, their pay, or the numbers they employ. These actions will have knock-on effects. As Werner has argued:

> *...the quantity of credit becomes the most important macroeconomic*
> *variable, delivering 'exogenous' (external) budget constraints to any*
> *particular market.*[203]

With a rationed and supply-determined credit market, it follows that adjusting interest rates is a policy that has a limited impact on credit-creation and hence the economy. With a limited role for reserve requirements and the abolition of bank credit guidance through the central bank, there are minimal external liquidity constraints on commercial banks. And finally, we have argued that capital adequacy rules are only a weak constraint on the creation of new commercial bank money, particularly with the advent of securitisation and other methods that allow banks to manipulate their balance sheets.

So, we can perhaps conclude the endogenous versus exogenous money debate in the following way. In modern economies where new money is created by the banking system, the supply of money is driven by credit creation. But credit creation is not driven by the demand for credit. Instead, the credit market is determined by the supply of credit. Credit is rationed and it is the quantity of credit supplied, rather than the price of credit, which will determine macro-economic outcomes. Without even perhaps being aware of it, banks are thus in a very powerful position. The total increase, or decrease, in the nation's money supply is the collective result of their individual lending and asset purchase decisions. In other words, because commercial banks ration and allocate credit, and they create new money in the process, they have a decisive influence over the allocation of new money in our economy.

5.7. Regulating bank credit directly: international examples

These facts suggest that the appropriate regulation of the total quantity of credit creation, and the quality of its use (i.e. the allocation of credit for different types of use) are key variables that economic policymakers should monitor and, indeed, seek to control. The quantity and allocation of credit across different uses will shape the economic landscape.

Indeed, during their history, almost all central banks have employed forms of direct credit regulation – variously called credit controls, the direction of credit, the guidance of credit, the framing of credit, window guidance, or moral suasion. We discussed the example of the UK in Chapter 2, Section 2.6.2.

---

* Series: 'Annual amounts outstanding of UK resident monetary financial institutions' sterling net lending, not seasonally adjusted'. Adjustments were made to figures on secured lending (code RPATBVX) to reflect changes in the Bank of England's reporting of covered bonds and securitised loans – see http://www.bankofengland.co.uk/mfsd/iadb/notesi-adb/Industrial.htm

but it is worth also examining other international examples in the twentieth century, in particular in Asia.

First implemented by the German Reichsbank in 1912, credit controls were copied by the Federal Reserve in the 1920s and had the greatest impact in economic history when adopted by the Japanese, Korean, and Taiwanese central banks in the early 1940s (during WWII) and then continued for many decades in the post-war era. Called 'window guidance' in these countries, the central bank would determine desired nominal GDP growth, then calculate the necessary amount of credit creation to achieve this, and then allocate this credit creation both across the various banks and types of banks, and across industrial sectors.

Unproductive credit creation was suppressed. Thus it was difficult or impossible to obtain bank credit for large-scale, purely speculative transactions, such as today's large-scale bank lending to hedge funds, as such financial credit creation would merely produce asset inflation and subsequent banking crises. Likewise, it was difficult to obtain consumer loans on a significant scale, as these would increase the demand for consumer goods, but not result in a direct increase in goods and services available, hence triggering consumer price inflation. Most bank credit was allocated to productive use, which meant either investment in plant and equipment to produce more goods, or investment to offer more services, or other forms of investment that enhanced productivity (such as the implementation of new technologies, processes, and know-how) – and often a combination of these. Such productive credit creation turned out to be the least inflationary, since not only was more money created but also more goods and services, and there was more value added.

The banks were quite willing to participate in such a system of credit guidance, because in return they also achieved unrivalled stability and a much greater degree of certainty concerning their market shares or even profits. Banks were recognised to be public utilities, and thus bonuses were also far more modest than, for instance, in the UK at the same time.

The World Bank recognised in a 1993 study that this mechanism of intervention in credit allocation was at the core of the East Asian Economic Miracle.[204] Deng Xiao Ping earlier recognised this and made Japanese-style window guidance the core of the Chinese economic reforms that led to decades of extremely high economic growth in China. While Western central banks have downplayed in public the importance and efficiency of such intervention in the credit market by the central bank (it seems not in line with the 'efficient market hypothesis' otherwise favoured in these countries' central banks and finance ministries), the Chinese central bank officially states that window guidance is one of its key monetary policy tools. Empirical research has shown that this is indeed the case.[205] Window guidance is also a key reason why the Chinese economy has not fallen victim to the Asian economic crisis or to the banking crisis of 2008.[*]

Detailed research on the efficacy of window guidance by the Bank of Japan has shown that this monetary policy tool has always worked extremely effectively (even when the goals set by the central bank were the wrong ones, such as the expansion of financial and speculative credit in the 1980s).[206] In other words, credit guidance is an effective tool, although this is no guarantee that the policy goals selected will be the right ones. Economic history thus provides evidence that that a simple regime of credit guidance, combined with adequate incentives (both carrots and sticks) for the banking system is an attractive avenue for delivering stable (and high) economic growth that is sustainable, and without recurring banking crises. Equally, this suggests that by severely limiting or entirely banning bank credit for transactions that do not contribute to GDP, asset bubbles and banking crises might be avoided. To be sure, such a measure would not stop speculation. Instead, it would not allow speculators to use the public privilege of money creation for their speculative transactions.

---

[*] However, it seems China went overboard with credit expansion in the aftermath of the Lehman collapse in 2008, expanding more than just productive credit, but instead also boosting financial credit. This seems to have created an asset bubble, and thus is likely to cause problems in the future, if not handled suitably.

6. Conclusions

6.1. Money: credit or commodity?

The historical overview of the origins of modern banking laid out in Chapter 2 illustrates that the majority of money in circulation in the UK is created as credit/debt by private sector banks.

Banks create new deposits through making loans, buying existing assists or by providing overdraft facilities which customers themselves turn in to deposits when they draw on them. These deposits are accepted by everyone, including the state, in payment for taxes. It is a simple step from here to say that banks create money. It is the ability of banks to create new money, independently of the state, which gave rise to capitalism and makes it distinctive. As political economist Geoffrey Ingham describes it, following Joseph Schumpeter:

> *The financing of production with money-capital in the form of newly created bank money uniquely specifies capitalism as a form of economic system. Enterprises, wage labour and market exchange existed to some small degree, at least, in many previous economic systems, but … their expansion into the dominant mode of production was made possible by the entirely novel institution of a money-producing banking system.*[207]

The promissory notes and bills of exchange issued by the goldsmiths and merchants of seventeenth-century London were backed by nothing other than a claim on future income: they were promises to pay. But these bills would always be limited in their scale whilst they remained essentially personalised contracts. When the British state, desperate for funds to meet the cost for foreign wars and basically unable to mint silver fast enough to do so, also began to borrow from goldsmiths (instead of issuing government money, as had been done during the tally sticks era), the opportunity arose for modern money to emerge. These creditors, determined that the sovereign not renege on his debts, helped to establish a bank with monopoly powers to accept their promissory notes at a discounted rate. As Ingham argues:

> *…the privately owned Bank of England transformed the sovereign's personal debt in to a public debt and then eventually, in to a public currency [...] The private money of the bill of exchange was lifted out from the private mercantile network and given a wider and more abstract monetary space based on impersonal trust and legitimacy.*[208]

Thus modern capitalism gave birth to a hierarchical form of regulatory control, with the central bank at the apex of the hierarchy, ensuring the continued link between the nominal value of commercial bank money and the real value of central bank money (Bank of England notes and coins). The hope was that the central bank could control the quantity of commercial bank money through its power of discounting and, as lender of last resort, rescue any bank which faced a run as depositors lost confidence by emergency issuance of central bank money ('printing money'). For short periods of time, the system appeared to be stable, most obviously during the 1950s and 1960s, with a fixed exchange rate and strict national and international credit controls in place.

But deregulation and developments in technology have now led us to a situation where commercial banks now completely dominate the creation of credit and hence the money supply, even though the acceptability of money is guaranteed by the state and the security of bank deposits backed ultimately by the tax-payer. In fact one could argue that demand deposits are even more liquid than pure cash, since today it is much easier and often cheaper to pay taxes and virtually every other regular debt (e.g. for utilities) by transferring demand deposits. Indeed if you do not have a bank account today, your life is considerably more complicated and expensive. Research has shown that lacking access to a bank account can lead to cumulative additional financial charges, excess interest and higher costs for energy and other utilities of up to £1,000 a year.[209]

6.2. What counts as money: drawing the line

Identifying what counts as money is not easy, as we saw in Chapter 3, because financial innovation means that when an instrument is defined and controlled as 'money', substitutes will be found to enable (tax) evasion: 'Goodhart's Law'.[210]

Such instruments include securities issued against loans made on the security of highly illiquid assets such as houses and derivatives – streams of future obligations to pay. Although never really considered as money, such instruments are increasingly traded in a money-like fashion, moved around the world at great speed and frequency by investment banks, hedge funds and other global financial actors. But as the financial crisis has revealed, their acceptability ultimately depends upon the strength of the credit-debtor relationship. When it became clear during the financial crisis that many of the mortgage-backed securities in the United States were based on sub-prime loans whose borrowers were likely to default, the result was a massive and systemic collapse of confidence between banks as these debts had been spread over such a wide range of banks' assets. So these mortgage-backed securities turned from being highly liquid and money-like, easily bought and sold, to being highly illiquid in a matter of days.

Expectations then become central to liquidity and 'money-ness': when expectations concerning future system-wide developments are stable and widely shared, then a wide spectrum of private liabilities will be regarded as liquid and will find a place in the portfolios of those units whose current operations generate a surplus of revenues over expenditures.[211] Thus liquidity itself becomes highly subjective, and the potential for system-wide collapse in liquidity increases.

A further difficulty in defining money arises from the tension between money's role as a means of exchange (where the more liquid the better) and its role as a store of value, where generally assets which are less liquid, such as homes, tend to hold their value more effectively, because of inflation.[212] It may be that different conceptions of money are partly driven by the relative importance that people place on the different functions of money – whether they consider its usefulness as a store of value to be the most important aspect, or its usefulness and availability as a means of exchange.

6.3. Implications of the credit theory of money

The implications of the credit model of money are profound. Rather than being neutral or a veil over the 'real' activities of the economy (trade, exchange, the use of land and labour), it becomes clear that money – as an abstract, impersonal claim on future resources – is a social and political construct. As such, its impacts are determined by whoever decides what it is (the unit of account), who issues it, how much of it is issued and how it is allocated.

The unit of account function continues to be determined primarily by the state, as it has been going back at least four thousand years.[213] It is able to do this simply because we live in societies where, even accepting the presence of vast efforts devoted to off-shoring and tax-haven activities, with vast stores of wealth that simply never see the state in any real sense, most of us have to make regular payments to the state in the form of taxation. If people (and firms) know they must make regular payments denominated in a certain way, it makes perfect sense to use such a denomination equally for their own transactions. The medium of exchange may change – credit cards, cheques, online payments – but the unit of account remains the same, otherwise money loses its power of acceptability.

So we can conclude by saying that money is really nothing more than a promise to pay. However, what distinguishes money from pure credit or, say, an IOU note, is its general acceptability. Promises to pay that are accepted as tax will tend to be the most widely accepted for private debts and exchanges as almost everyone needs to make regular tax payments. The nature of the credit-debt relationship is abstract rather than specific.[214] As American economist Hyman Minsky has pointed out, 'anyone can create money, the problem is getting it accepted'.[215] Since banks are the accountants of the economy, through whose computers the vast majority of all transactions are booked, they are uniquely placed to get their money – created though granting credit – accepted. Part of the widespread acceptance may have been due to the fact that the general public is simply not aware that banks do indeed create the money supply.

People accept and hold money not because of its intrinsic value as a commodity but because of guarantees regarding its future re-exchangeability; the 'satisfaction... of the holder does not depend on possession per se, but on possession with a view to future use for payment'.[216]

Future exchangeability is guaranteed by the state in three key respects:

1. through its acceptability to pay taxes;

2. by tax-payer-funded insurance of bank deposits, and;

3. by tax-payer-funded guarantees that banks will be bailed out if they get into trouble.

We can then say that all money is credit but not all credit is money. Schumpeter[217] recognised that what is required is a credit theory of money rather than a monetary theory of credit. And, whilst no definition is perfect, Geoffrey Ingham's conception of money, which follows Keynes and Schumpeter, seems appropriate: money is 'a social relation of abstract value defined by a sovereign unit of account'.[218] Rather than 'appearing' or being 'called forth' by the natural operations of the market, money is in fact issued into circulation as a social relation of credit and debt between the state and its citizens.[219] As such, it can be fairly accurately accounted for, when measuring credit creation in the banking system and credit creation by the central bank.[220]

6.4. Questions to consider

So we have found a paradox at the heart of our monetary system; it is the state that essentially determines what money is and underwrites its value, and yet it is predominately commercial banks that create it. In deciding who receives credit, banks determine broadly how it is spent within the economy, whether on consumption, buying existing assets or productive investment. They play a vital macroeconomic role.

This raises some serious questions about public and private interest:

- If the state's role is so crucial in determining what money is, why does it seem to have such trouble controlling the money supply, as the difficulties of monetarist policies in the 1980s demonstrated?

- Why has it been unable to prevent the financial and banking crises we have seen over the past eight centuries?[221]

- Ought the state have more power to determine how much money is issued in to the economy and for what purpose?

- If banks have been awarded the public privilege to create the money supply (i.e. the money creation process has been privatised) should they not also be given certain obligations to ensure that this enormous power is used mainly for activities that contribute to the common good? Or should banks continue to be allowed to use this public privilege for what appears to be their short-term benefits, when indeed banks apparently cannot be trusted to look even after their own medium- to long-term interests.

- Does it make sense for shareholder-owned and profit-driven banks to have such powers of credit creation whilst financial institutions, such as credit unions, for example, which are owned cooperatively and have primarily a social purpose, are restricted in their credit-creating powers?[222]

- Have central banks been given the right monetary policy targets, the right mandates, and the right powers to carry out these tasks? Ultimately, banking crises are due to credit-driven asset bubbles. But it should be the job of monetary policy to prevent these. Should the consumer inflation target be replaced or augmented with targets for asset price inflation?

- Should credit guidance, including the suppression of credit creation for speculative purposes, be reintroduced into the UK monetary policy toolset? Could this be one of the powers of the new Financial Policy Committee? And should such measures be combined with further policies to encourage productive credit creation (such as giving banks incentives to lend to small and medium-sized enterprises, for instance through rules about bank bonuses),[223] and policies that reshape the banking sector, such as encouraging more small, local or regional banks that are incentivised to develop long-term local relationships with customers

- Does it make sense regularly to land the tax-payers with the costs of bankers' mistakes, without apparent punishment or serious deterrent for the bankers? Should the government and the central bank consider less costly alternatives of dealing with banking crises that do not burden the taxpayer with huge debts? For example, could the central bank, in its capacity as lender of last resort, be the one to purchase non-performing assets from banks at face value, and keep them on its balance sheet? Should the UK government set up national banks able to create credit at zero or very low rates of interest for specific infrastructure projects for example?[*] Should the restrictions imposed upon direct government credit creation by the Maastricht Treaty be reviewed?

It is disappointing that so few of these questions have been addressed by the Independent Commission on Banking and other national and international processes examining reform of the financial system. Indeed, the ICB reports included scant and inaccurate discussion of the key role played by banks in creating new money.

6.4.1. Is this system safe enough, and is it useful?

The power of commercial banks to create new money also has many important implications for economic prosperity and financial stability, and we highlight four that are relevant to the reforms of the banking system under discussion at the time of writing:

1. Although useful in other ways, capital adequacy requirements do not constrain money creation, and therefore do not constrain the expansion of banks' balance sheets in aggregate. In other words, they are ineffective in preventing credit booms and their associated asset price bubbles

2. Credit is rationed by banks, and the primary determinant of how much they lend is not interest rates, but confidence that the loan will be repaid and confidence in the liquidity and solvency of other banks and the system as a whole

---

[*] See the proposals in *The Green New Deal* (2008), **nef** (the new economics foundation) and the Green New Deal Group, accessible at http://www.neweconomics.org/projects/green-new-deal [accessed 4th September 2011]

3. Banks in effect decide where to allocate new credit in the economy. The incentives that they currently face lead them to favour credit creation for the purchase of existing assets, rather than lending for investment in the creation of new assets. New money is more likely to be channelled into property and financial speculation than to small businesses and manufacturing, with profound economic consequences.

4. Fiscal policy does not in itself result in an expansion of the money supply. Indeed the government has in practice no direct involvement in the money creation and allocation process. This is little known but has as important impact on the effectiveness of fiscal policy and the role of the government in the economy.

6.4.2. And is it really the best available alternative?

We have seen that some answers may lie in a mistaken understanding of money's nature by successive sovereigns and governments. In Chapter 2, we showed how the government's need for funds combined with its belief that only gold and silver could be used as the basis for money gave rise to the particular institutional arrangements we have today. The misunderstanding of money as a commodity rather than a creditor/debtor relationship has so dominated the imagination of our leaders and economists that they have allowed the development of a monetary policy regime that, despite repeated crises, remains steadfast.

But as various examples show, including banknotes issued by the Treasury during WWI, a system where money creation is almost entirely in the hands of commercial banks is not inevitable.

The purpose of this book, however, is not to examine comprehensively the consequences, good and bad, of our current monetary and banking system. Neither is it to appraise or recommend alternatives other than simply to observe that alternatives are possible and do exist. Our purpose is to accurately describe our current system, and some of the implications for regulating it, in the hope of a better informed debate about whether and how the system might be reformed.

The basic analysis of this book is neither radical nor new, although we hope it provides a coherent and comprehensive contemporary account. In fact, central banks around the world support the same description of where new money comes from. And yet many naturally resist the notion that commercial banks can really create new money.

We conclude that commercial banks clearly do create money and allocate purchasing power and this book explains in some detail the mechanics of the process. There is no deeper mystery, as Galbraith suggested, and we must not allow our mind to be repelled. Only then can we properly address the much more significant question: of all the possible alternative ways in which we *could* create new money, is this really the best?

Appendix 1: The central bank's interest rate regime

A1.1. Setting interest rates – demand-driven central bank money

The Bank of England's Monetary Policy Committee (MPC) meets once a month in order to set the interest rate which it judges will enable the inflation target to be met. However, this interest rate (known as the **policy rate**) is not the interest rate at which you or I would be able to borrow from high street banks. Instead, it aims to influence the interest rate at which banks lend to each other on the interbank market, which in turn will influence the rates offered by banks to customers.[224]

From 2006 up to 2009, the Bank of England aimed to set the interest rate through a mechanism known as the **corridor system**. Under this system, banks set their own reserve targets (the amount of central bank reserves they would plan to hold to enable all payments) every month, and borrow these reserves from the central bank using repos (Section 3.6).*

If a bank found itself with reserves in excess of its target, then it could either lend them to other banks on the interbank market or deposit them at the Bank of England, and receive interest on them at a rate known as the **deposit rate**. If a bank needed additional reserves, it could borrow in the interbank market or overnight from the Bank of England, paying interest at the **lending rate**.

The deposit rate was set slightly below, and the lending rate slightly above, the policy rate (Figure A1). The interbank interest rate was unlikely to fall below the deposit rate, as, if so, it would be more profitable for a bank to simply deposit the reserves at the Bank of England rather than lend them to another bank. Equally, a bank would be unlikely to borrow from another bank at a rate higher than that which they could borrow from the Bank of England using the lending facility.[225] This created the aforementioned corridor around the policy rate (Figure A1).

As mentioned, the banks had to set reserve targets. Only if the banks' reserve balances on average over the month fell within a relatively narrow range around those targets, would they be paid interest on them at the policy rate. Outside

---

* The 'repo rate' – the rate which the banks borrow reserves from the central bank, was set equal to the policy rate. This meant that as long as the banks hit their reserve targets, there was no cost to the banks of holding reserves, and no 'tax' on the banking system as a whole. Fisher, P. (2011). *Recent developments in the sterling monetary framework.* London: Bank of England, p. 9.

Figure A1: Corridor system of reserves.[226]

this range, surplus reserves would not receive interest, and there were penalties for failing to meet their target, creating incentives for banks to manage their liquidity effectively. [227]

Students of economics might find this description of how the Bank of England sets interest rates rather confusing, with most textbook models involving the central bank adjusting the quantity of reserves (through open market operations) and thus changing the interest rate at which the supply of central bank reserves intersects with the demand for central bank reserves. However, as Paul Tucker, Deputy Governor of the Bank of England, states: 'Neither in the past nor in the current review have we even briefly entertained the notion that this is realistic.'[228]

He goes on to say that, under a reserves averaging scheme:

> *Open market operations will not be used to inject a quantity of reserves according to a plan for the path of the monetary base. And they will not be used directly to adjust the quantity of base money to bring about the desired level of short-term interest rates. In other words, base money comprises neither a target nor an instrument of policy. Rather, the role of OMOs will be to satisfy the system's targeted level of reserves over the maintenance period as a whole.*[229]

Figure A2: The floor system of reserves.[230]

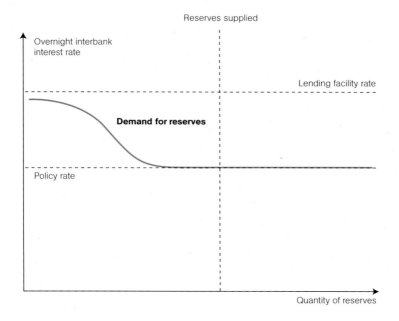

A1.2.   **Setting interest rates – supply-driven central bank money**

The corridor system and reserve targeting was suspended in March 2009, switching to a **floor system**. This followed the decision of the MPC to embark upon the purchase of financial assets funded through the **creation of central bank money**, popularly known as **quantitative easing**. The bank ended up creating £200 billion worth of central bank reserves, and used them predominantly to buy government securities (a small amount of corporate securities were also purchased).

So the banking system now holds central bank reserves far in excess of the reserve targets they previously set, and interest is paid on these reserves at the policy rate. Due to these excess reserves, the need for banks to borrow from each other on the interbank market has been greatly diminished, and thus the interbank rate closely matches the policy rate. Hence the UK has recently moved from a system of demand-driven central bank money (the reserves targeting scheme), to supply-driven central bank money (the floor scheme) (Figure A2).

Under the floor system, banks have excess reserves; however, it is unclear whether this has had any impact on banks' lending to customers. Since the financial crisis, the banks' confidence has been severely diminished. Thus it appears to be banks' levels of confidence, rather than the level of reserves, which is dictating bank willingness to lend and create new money.

APPENDIX 2: THE UK DEBT MANAGEMENT ACCOUNT 2008–2010

Assets	2010 £m	2009 £m	2008 £m
Cash and balances at the Bank of England	420	714	500
Loans and advances to banks	44,187	34,863	14,206
Securities held for trading	924	4,841	17
Derivative financial instruments	58	1	82
Investment securities classified as available-for-sale:			
Of which: 1. UK Government gilt-edged securities for use as collateral subject to sale and repurchase agreements	20,814	25,867	12,038
2. UK Government gilt-edged securities for use as collateral not pledged	65,685	67,300	17,002
Total (1+2)	86,499	93,167	29,040
3. Other UK Government gilt-edged securities	52,275	54,280	123
4. Treasury bills	176,108	205,148	-
Total (1+2+3+4)	314,882	352,595	29,163
Other assets	18	72	6
Total assets before deposit at National Loans Fund	**360,489**	**393,086**	**43,974**
Deposit at National Loans Fund	28,511	48,967	49,140
Total assets	**389,000**	**442,053**	**93,114**
Liabilities			
Deposits by banks	15,355	29,343	12,162
Due to government customers	56,478	66,148	62,287
Derivative financial instruments	27	257	331
Treasury bills in issue	62,973	43,895	17,441
Other liabilities	128	9	4
Total liabilities before funding by National Loans Fund	**134,961**	**139,652**	**92,225**
Advance from National Loans Fund	242,127	292,166	-
Revaluation reserve	4,137	7,844	1,085
Income and expenditure account	7,775	2,391	196
Total funding by National Loans Fund	**254,039**	**302,401**	**889**
Total liabilities	**389,000**	**442,053**	**93,114**

Source: Annual Report and Accounts 2009/2010 of the United Kingdom Debt Management Office and the Debt Management Account, page 84.

APPENDIX 3: ASSETS AND LIABILITIES OF THE EXCHANGE EQUALISATION ACCOUNT 2008–2010

Statement of Financial Position on:	31 March 2010	31 March 2009	1 April 2008
	£ millions	£ millions Restated	£ millions Restated
Assets			
Cash and balances at central banks and the Government Banking Service	553	435	778
Items in the course of collection from banks	783	231	284
Treasury bills	132	1,606	475
Debt securities	23,885	24,146	21,782
Derivative financial assets	863	1,286	774
Reverse repurchase agreements	4,001	299	3,484
Holdings of IMF Special Drawing Rights	9,158	301	176
Gold	7,334	6,377	4,686
Other financial assets	105	5	3
Total assets	**46,814**	**34,686**	**32,442**
Liabilities			
Deposits by banks	36	40	92
Items in the course of transmission to banks	1,008	253	403
Debt securities - short positions	632	259	479
Derivative financial liabilities	1,890	4,143	2,086
Repurchase agreements	2,907	1,907	2,935
Other financial liabilities	4	2	7
SDR allocation	10,144	1,996	1,583
Liability to the National Loans Fund	30,193	26,086	24,857
Total liabilities	**46,814**	**34,686**	**32,442**

Reproduced from: HM Treasury. *Exchange Equalisation Account: Report and Accounts 2009-10*

APPENDIX 4: FOREIGN EXCHANGE PAYMENT, TRADE AND SPECULATION

A4.1.   Trade and speculation

Businesses require foreign exchange services in order to buy, sell, and invest in different countries. An American car company (say General Motors) that owns a factory in the UK will need to convert dollars to pounds, and vice versa. However, this creates a problem – if exchange rates can fluctuate, then it may be difficult for General Motors to know its costs (in dollars) when agreeing contracts. For instance, imagine at the beginning of each year General Motors draws up a contract with the UK factory, agreeing to pay wages to its staff totalling £10 million. With an exchange rate of £1 = $1.50 the wages will cost General Motors $15 million. However, no sooner than the contract is signed the exchange rate changes to £1 = $2. General Motors now has to pay $20 million in order to honour the contract. Although an extra $5 million is unlikely to be a problem for a business the size of General Motors, large fluctuations in exchange rates can be catastrophic for smaller businesses.

General Motors can protect itself from currency risk through a process known as **hedging**. The two most common forms of hedging in the foreign exchange market are **forward contracts** and **options**. A forward contract allows General Motors to lock in the current exchange rate, so that whatever the exchange rate is at the end of the year, it can still exchange its pounds for dollars at the rate set in the contract (say £1 = $1.5). Options contracts are similar, but instead they give General Motors the right, but not the obligation, to exchange currencies at the exchange rate set in the contract. Although hedging can reduce the risk arising from exchange rate fluctuations, it is possible that General Motors might find itself in a worse position than if it hadn't made the forward contract. For example, if, when the time comes to exchange currencies, the exchange rate is £1 = $1, then General Motors could have paid its workers with just $10 million rather than the $15 million required when the exchange rate is £1 = $1.50 – a loss of $5 million.

But whom is General Motors making this contract with? One possibility would be a UK business that wishes to pay for something in dollars at the end of the year, and is also worried about currency risk. Another would be a speculator, who wishes to bet on the outcome of exchange rate fluctuations. For instance, a speculator may enter into the contract with General Motors, agreeing to receive $15 million in exchange for £10 million next year, at an exchange rate of £1 = $1.50. If the exchange rate does not change, then the speculator neither gains nor loses from the exchange. However if, come the day of the exchange, the exchange rate stands at £1 = $1, the speculator can borrow £10 million at a UK bank, exchange it for $15 million with General Motors, then swap the $15 million back into pounds. At an exchange rate of £1 = $1 the speculator ends up with £15 million – a profit of £5 million. However, if the exchange rate went the other way then the speculator would end up with a loss!

Box A1. Foreign exchange instruments

Foreign exchange transactions can be broken down into their component parts, which are spot transactions and three different types of 'plain vanilla derivatives' (forwards, swaps, and options), as well as other foreign exchange (forex) products:

Spots: The spot transaction is the most widely known forex transaction. A spot transaction is an exchange of two currencies at a rate agreed on the date of the contract, with the currency being delivered (electronically) within two business days. On average, spot transactions accounted for $1,490 billion a day in 2010.

Forwards: Forwards are similar to spot transactions; however, unlike in the spot market, the currency is delivered more than two business days after the contract is agreed. This allows participants to 'lock in' an exchange rate for a future transaction, thus eliminating uncertainty over fluctuations in the values of the currencies. On average, forwards accounted for $475 billion a day in 2010.

Currency swaps: Currency swaps allow for the exchange of two currencies on a specific date at a set exchange rate, and then a reversal of the swap on a future date, usually at a different exchange rate. Commonly, this is a combination of a spot trade with a forward trade of opposite direction (e.g. sell CHF 100,000 and buy EUR spot; buy CHF 100,000 and sell EUR 30 days forward). On average, currency swaps accounted for $1,765 billion a day in 2010.

Foreign interest rate swaps: Such a swap is actually about swapping interest payments in different currencies. They allow the exchange of streams of interest payments between counterparties for a period of time, with the exchange of principle at a pre agreed exchange rate at maturity. On average, currency swaps accounted for $43 billion a day in 2010.

Options: Currency options give the holders the right (which they do not have to exercise) to acquire or sell foreign currency at a specified price for a certain period of time. On average, options and related forex products accounted for $207 billion a day in 2010.

Figure A3: Amount of foreign currency settled per day by settlement method (2006).[231]

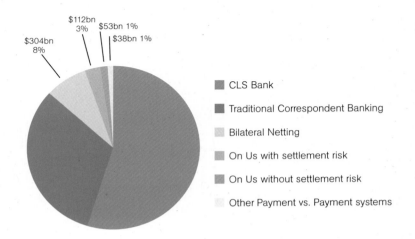

Legend:
- CLS Bank
- Traditional Correspondent Banking
- Bilateral Netting
- On Us with settlement risk
- On Us without settlement risk
- Other Payment vs. Payment systems

$304bn 8%, $112bn 3%, $53bn 1%, $38bn 1%

A4.2. The foreign exchange payment system

All but the very largest organisations will not participate directly in forex markets. Instead their banks will facilitate any instruction to exchange one currency for another on their behalf. So how do banks convert one currency to another? Obviously they do not send bundles of cash around the world. Forex transactions are therefore settled electronically, in one of six different ways.

A4.2.1. Traditional correspondent banking

Traditional correspondent banking (also known as gross non-payment versus payment (PVP) settlement) is, as its name suggests, the traditional method for settling forex transactions. In 2006, it settled around 32 per cent of all forex transactions, or $1,224 billion a day. This is down from 87 per cent of all forex trades settled in 1997.[232] To understand why traditional correspondent banking has declined, we must first understand how it works.

Imagine RBS engages in a spot trade with HSBC, in which it is selling yen for US dollars. Furthermore imagine that neither HSBC nor RBS have access to either the American or Japanese payment system (i.e. neither of them has an account with the FED or the Bank of Japan). However, HSBC has a bank account[233] with a Japanese Bank (that has access to the Japanese payment system) as well as an account with an American Bank (that has access to the American payment system). These are HSBC's 'correspondent banks'. RBS also has correspondent banks in both America and Japan (Figure A3).

After RBS and HSBC strike the trade, RBS sends an instruction to its correspondent in Japan, asking the latter to send the yen to HSBCs correspondent there. RBS's Japanese correspondent executes this instruction by debiting the account that RBS holds with it and sending the yen to HSBCs Japanese correspondent via the Japanese payment system. After HSBC's Japanese correspondent has received the funds, it credits them to HSBC's account and informs HSBC that they have arrived.

In parallel, HSBC settles its side of the trade by a similar process in which it instructs its correspondent in the United States (HSBC USA) to send US dollars to RBS's American correspondent. [234]

There are major risks involved in using traditional correspondent banking to settle forex transactions, one of which is Herstatt risk (a form of settlement risk). Herstatt risk is the risk that one party to a forex trade pays out the currency it has sold, but does not receive the currency it has bought. Its name comes from the Herstatt Bank, which was forced into liquidation on 26 June 1974 by German regulators, because of a lack of income and capital to cover liabilities that were due. Before being closed, Herstatt Bank had received payments of Deutsche Marks which it had arranged to exchange for dollars (which were to be paid out by Herstatt's US nostro[235]) when the American payment system opened. However, the bank was closed before the American payment system opened, and thus the dollars were never sent. Therefore

Figure A4: Foreign exchange using correspondent banking.

Herstatt risk occurs primarily due to problems in coordinating the timing of the payment of two currencies in different payment systems.

The reason for the decline in traditional correspondent banking (a non-payment versus a payment system) is primarily due to the advent of payment versus payments systems such as Continuous Linked Settlement (CLS) Bank. Payment versus payment systems eliminate Herstatt risk by ensuring that both parties have paid in to a third party before either bank receives a payout. These are described in more detail below.

A4.2.2. Bilateral netting

Bilateral netting is a variant on traditional correspondent banking, and helps to limit settlement risk and credit risk. Rather than settle the gross value of all payments between two banks, netting arrangements permit banks to offset trades against each other so that only the net amount in each currency is paid or received by each institution. At the end of an agreed time period (usually a day), each counterparty will make a single payment to the other counterparty in each of the currencies in which it has a net debt, and receive payment in each of the currencies in which it has a net credit. This is particularly useful when two counterparties transact, or plan to transact forex regularly.[236]

A4.2.2.1. Payment versus payment systems: the case of CLS Bank

The CLS (continuous linked settlement) Bank was launched in 2002 by 70 of the world's leading financial service institutions. Since then it has become the largest forex settlement system, with a 58 per cent market share of global forex trading activity by value in 2010 (up from 55 per cent in 2006). However, CLS Bank currently only settles in 17 currencies* – for these currencies their market share is 68 per cent.[237] The CLS Bank was created primarily to eliminate Herstatt risk. It does this by using a payment versus payment (PVP) system, which settles both sides of a forex trade simultaneously.

A4.2.2.2. Stylised example of how CLS works [238,239]

CLS works in a similar way to traditional correspondent banking, but with an additional step. For CLS to work each member of CLS has to have a single multi-currency account with CLS Bank, and CLS must maintain an account with each of the 17 central banks for which it provides currency settlement services. In the UK CLS bank is a member of CHAPS and therefore CLS Bank

---

* These are: US Dollar, Euro, UK Pound, Japanese Yen, Swiss Franc, Canadian Dollar, Australian Dollar, Swedish Krona, Danish Krone, Norwegian Krone, the Singapore Dollar, the Hong Kong Dollar, the New Zealand Dollar, the Korean Won, the South African Rand, the Israeli Shekel and the Mexican Peso.

International has a settlement account within the Bank of England's RTGS system.[240]

After RBS and HSBC strike the trade, RBS sends an instruction to its correspondent in Japan, asking the latter to send the yen to HSBC's CLS account. RBS's Japanese correspondent executes this instruction by debiting the account that RBS holds with it and sending the yen to HSBC's CLS account via the Japanese payment system. In parallel, HSBC settles its side of the trade by a similar process in which it instructs its correspondent in the United States to send US dollars to RBSs CLS account.

Once CLS receives RBS's yen payment in its Japanese reserve account at the Bank of Japan, and HSBC's dollar payment in its reserve account at the FED, it completes the transaction by sending dollars to RBS's American correspondent and yen to HSBC's American correspondent. Herstatt risk is eliminated as CLS waits till it receives both RBS's yen and HSBC's dollars of funds before paying out.

If either bank fails to pay the money into CLS, then CLS can simply return the money of the bank that did pay in. However, this may not be necessary, as CLS Bank also has committed standby lines of credit with major banks for each currency it settles. Therefore, in Figure A3, if RBS fails to pay in yen (e.g. due to a lack of liquidity), CLS can simply take HSBC's dollars, exchange them for yen with its standby bank in Japan, then give this yen to HSBC. In this way Herstatt risk is eliminated and liquidity risk has been reduced (although not eliminated as the standby banks credit lines are finite).[241]

This example is simplified. In reality, banks submit huge numbers of payment instructions each day, although crucially all the payment instructions must be received by CLS before 6:30am Central European Time (CET) (see Figure A4). By requiring banks to submit their payment instructions before they have to pay in, CLS can net these amounts against each other. For example, a bank may have arranged several forex transactions with various counterparties, and as a result submits pay in instructions to CLS totalling £20 million. However, as a result of another set of forex trades it is scheduled to receive pay outs totalling £19 million. Thus, by determining the funding requirements of each bank on a 'multilaterally netted basis', the bank in question is required to pay in just £1 million. In reality the savings are much bigger. For every $1 trillion of value settled only $50 billion is required in liquidity – a 95 per cent reduction in funding requirements. In addition, netting also reduces the in-payments by 99.75 per cent, with an average of only 26 payments per day regardless of the value of the payments.[242]

A4.3. *On us, with and without risk*

On us settlement refers to forex settlement where both legs of the forex trade are conducted on the books of a single institution. This requires a bank to be a member of both countries' payment systems for the currencies in which it is settling. As such it does not require any movement of money between banks, as the bank simply debits and credits the relevant accounts in each country. On us comes in two forms:

1. *Without settlement risk:* Where the crediting of currency to the selling account is *conditional* on the debiting of currency from the buying account, for instance because both the buy and sell accounts are credited and debited simultaneously.

2. *With settlement risk:* Where the crediting of currency to the selling account is *not conditional* on the debiting of currency from the buying account. This could be due to the relevant RTGS systems not being open at the same time, forcing one party to the transaction to pay in first.[243]

A4.4. *Other payment versus payment settlement methods*

CLS Bank is not the only payment versus payment system. Hong Kong has local RTGS systems in Hong Kong Dollars (HKD), US dollars (USD) and euro. In September 2000 the Hong Kong Dollar and US dollar RTGS systems were linked together. This was followed by linking the euro RTGS system to the HKD and USD system in April 2003. Finally, in November 2006, this system was linked to Malaysia's ringgit RTGS system.

The system works in the following way. The two parties to a forex transaction simply submit their payment instructions to the RTGS system, using a code to identify to the RTGS system that the payments are for PVP settlement. Once both instructions are matched against each other and the funds are available for settlement, the two RTGS systems will pay out each currency simultaneously, thus eliminating Herstatt risk.

Figure A5: CLS Bank operational timeline

Ongoing submission of instructions	Settlement cycle	Funding (Pay-In and Pay-Out processes)
up to 06:30 CET	07:00–09:00 CET	09:00–12:00 CET

Funding and settlement takes place during a five-hour window when the opening times of the relevant RTGS systems overlap and are open to send and receive funds.

Submit instructions	Funding and Settlement	Execution	Funding (Pay-In and Pay-Out processes)
Settlement Members submit payment instructions directly to the CLS system for matching. Instructions can be submitted up to 06:30 Central European Time (CET)* for each settlement date.

At 06:30 CET each Settlement Member receives its final net pay-in schedule for the day. | Settlement Members pay in net funds based on the 06:30 CET schedule to the CLS Bank account at the relevant central bank.

CLS Bank settles each pair of matched payment instructions individually on a gross basis.

Funding and settlement processing begins at 07:00 CET. | Between 07:00 and 09:00 CET, CLS Bank continuously receives funds from Settlement Members, settles instructions across its books and pays out funds to Settlement Members until settlement is complete. Instructions that cannot immediately settle remain in the queue and are continually revisited.

Settlement is normally completed by 08:30 CET | The funding and payout process continues until 10:00 CET for Asia- Pacific currencies and until 12:00 CET for European and North American currencies.

Between 09:00 and 12:00 CET the pay-ins and pay-outs are completed. All funds will have been disbursed back to eligible Settlement Members by 12:00 CET, ensuring the efficient use of liquidity. |

The CLS operational timeline applies to CLS Settlement Members only. User Members and third parties settling in CLS may operate by a different funding timeline as agreed with their Settlement Member.

* The agreed best practice is to settle same day instructions outside CLS after 00:00 CET

Reproduced from: CLS Bank. About us. Available at: http://www.cls-group.com/Publications/CLS%20About%20Us.pdf

ENDNOTES

1   Galbraith, J. K. (1975). *Money: Whence it came, where it went*. London: Penguin, pp.18–19.

2   McKenna, R. (1928). *Postwar Banking Policy*. p.93

3   Keynes, J. M. (1930). *Preface to A Treatise on Money*, 3 vols, pvi-vii.

4   ESCP Europe/Cobden Centre. (June 2010). *Public attitudes to banking*. Retrieved from www.cobdencentre.org

5   Independent Commission on Banking. (2010). Interim paper: Consultation on reform options, pp.16, paragraph 8, Retrieved from http://s3-eu-west-1.amazonaws.com/htcdn/Interim-Report-110411.pdf

6   Defoe, D. (1690). *Essay on Projects* (London), quoted in Davies, G. (2002). *A History of Money*. Wales: University of Wales Press, p. 251.

7   Schumpeter, J. (1994/1954.) *History of Economic Analysis*. London: Allen & Union, p. 1114. Quoted in Werner, R. (2005). *New Paradigm in Macroeconomics*. Basingstoke: Palgrave Macmillan, p.189.

8   ESCP Europe. (2010). *op. cit.*

9   *Ibid.*

10   Adapted from Werner, R.A. (2005). *New Paradigm in Macroeconomics*. Basingstoke: Palgrave Macmillan, p. 150.

11   Independent Commission on Banking. (2010). Issues Paper: Call for Evidence, pp.144–145, Retrieved from http://bankingcommission.independent.gov.uk/wp-content/uploads/2010/07/Issues-Paper-24-September-2010.pdf

12   Bank of England statistics for the M4 measure of broad money supply. Calculated by removing Notes & Coins from M4 and calculating the ratio.

13   King, M. (1994). The transition mechanism of monetary policy. *Bank of England Quarterly Bulletin*, August 1994, p. 264. Retrieved from http://www.bankofengland.co.uk/publications/quarterlybulletin/qb940301.pdf

14   Berry, S., Harrison, R., Thomas, R., de Weymarn, I. (2007). Interpreting movements in Broad Money. *Bank of England Quarterly Bulletin* 2007 Q3, p. 377. Retrieved from http://www.bankofengland.co.uk/publications/quarterlybulletin/qb070302.pdf

15   Burgess, S., Janssen, N. (2007). Proposals to modify the measurement of broad money in the United Kingdom: A user-consultation. *Bank of England Quarterly Bulletin* 2007 Q3, p. 402. Retrieved from http://www.bankofengland.co.uk/publications/quarterlybulletin/qb070304.pdf

16   Berry *et al.* (2007) *op. cit.* p. 378.

17   Tucker, P. (2008). 'Money and Credit: Banking and the macroeconomy', speech given at the monetary policy and markets conference, 13 December 2007, *Bank of England Quarterly Bulletin* 2008, Q1, pp. 96–106. Retrieved from http://www.bankofengland.co.uk/publications/speeches/2007/speech331.pdf

18   'Minutes of Proceedings and Evidence Respecting the Bank of Canada' (1939). Committee on Banking and Commerce, Ottawa. Government Printing Bureau, quoted in Rowbotham, M. (1998). *The Grip of Death*. Oxford: John Carpenter Publishing, p. 12.

19   ECB. (2000). 'Domestic payments in Euroland: commercial and central bank money'. Speech by Tommaso Padoa-Schioppa, Member of the Executive Board of the European central bank, at the European Commission Round-Table *Establishing a Single Payment Area: State of Play and Next Steps*, Brussels, 9 November 2000, quoted in Werner, R., (2009). *Can credit unions create credit? An Analytical Evaluation of a Potential Obstacle to the Growth of Credit Unions*. Southampton: Centre for Banking, Finance and Sustainable Development, Discussion Paper Series, No. 2/09, p. 5.

20 Nichols, D. M. (1992/1961). *Modern Money Mechanics: A workbook on Bank Reserves and Deposit Expansion*. Chicago: Federal Reserve Bank of Chicago. Retrieved from http://www.archive.org/stream/ ModernMoneyMechanics/MMM#page/n1/mode/2up

21 Bundesbank. (2009). Geld und Geldpolitik, as cited and translated by Werner, R.A. (2009). Topics in Monetary Economics, Lecture Slides for Master in Money and Finance. Frankfurt: Goethe University.

22 See Association of British Credit Unions Limited, 'Legislative Reform Order re-laid in Parliament, http://www.abcul.org/media-and-research/news/view/151

23 Werner (2005). *op. cit.,* p. 175.

24 Tucker (2007). *op. cit.*

25 For a similar visual approach to describing money see: Credit Suisse (5 May 2009). *Market Focus - Long Shadows: Collateral Money, Asset Bubbles and Inflation*, p. 7.

26 Bank of England statistics, 2006, ratio of M4 (broad money) to M0 (base money – notes and coins plus Bank of England reserves).

27 Simmel, G. (2004/1907). *The Philosophy of Money*, 3rd Edition. London: Routledge, p.148.

28 Ferguson, N. (2008). *The Ascent of Money: A Financial History of the World*. London: Penguin, p. 31.

29 Other functions commonly ascribed to money include a 'standard for deferred payments' and 'common measure of value'. Davies, G. (2002). *A History of Money*. Cardiff: University of Wales Press, p. 27.

30 Jevons, W. S. (1896/1875). *Money and the Mechanism of Exchange*. New York: Appleton and Company.

31 Mill, J. S. (1871). *Principles of Political Economy*, p.341.

32 Menger, C. (1892). On the Origins of Money. Economic Journal **2:** 239–255.

33 Jevons (1896/1875). *op. cit.*

34 Radford, R. A. (1945). The Economic Organisation of a POW Camp. *Econometrica*, Volume 12.

35 Schumpeter (1994/1954). *op. cit.* p. 277.

36 Walras, L. (1954/1874). Elements of Pure Economics. London: Allen & Unwin.

37 Pigou, A. C. (1949). *The Veil of Money*. London: Macmillan.

38 Marshall, A. (1996/1899). 'Evidence to the Indian Currency Committee' in Marshall, A. (n.d.). Correspondence of Alfred Marshall, Economist, Vol: II, 1891–1902 at the Summit. Cambridge: Cambridge University Press.

39 Pigou (1949). *op. cit.*

40 Sidrauski, M. (1967). Rational choice and patterns of growth in a monetary economy. *American Economic Review* 57(2): 534–544.

41 Clower, R. (1967). A reconsideration of the microfoundations of money. Western Economics Journal. Retrieved from http://www.carlostrub.ch/sites/default/files/Clower1967.pdf, in Walker D. (ed.) Money and Markets, Cambridge: Cambridge University Press, pp. 81–99; Hahn, F. (1965). On some problems of proving the existence of an equilibrium in a monetary economy, in Hahn, F., Brechling, F.P.R. (eds), Theory of Interest Rates, London: Macmillan; Lapavitsas, C. (2005). The emergence of money in commodity exchange, or money as monopolist of the ability to buy. Review of Political Economy 17(4): 549–569.

42 Marx, K. (1976/1867). *Capital, Vol. 1,* Harmondsworth: Penguin.

43 Minsky, H.P. (1986/2008). Stabilizing an Unstable Economy. Yale: McGrawhill, pp. 159–160.

44 Dodd, N. (1994). *The Sociology of Money,* Cambridge: Polity Press, p. 12.

45 Keynes, J. M. (2008/1936). *The General Theory of Employment, Interest and Money.* BNPublishing

46 Werner (2005). *op. cit.* pp.17–18.

47 Keynes, J. K. (1930). A Treatise on Money: Vol 1 A Pure Theory of Money, Chapter 1.

48 Goodhart (1998). *op. cit.*

49   Smithin, J. (2000). Introduction in *What is money?* London: Routledge, pp.1–16.

50   Ingham, G. (2004). *The Nature of Money.* Cambridge: Polity Press.

51   Leyshon, A., Thrift, N. (1997). *Money/Space: Geographies of Monetary Transformation*, Routledge: London;

52   Mellor, M. (2010). *The Future of Money: From Financial Crisis to Public Resource*, Chapter 1. London: Pluto.

53   Davies (2002). *op. cit.* pp. 50–55.

54   *Ibid.* pp. 50–51 quoting from Orsingher, R. (1964). *Banks of the World: A History and Analysis.* Paris: viii.

55   Davies (2002). *op .cit.* p. 50.

56   Innes, A.M. (1913). What is Money? *Banking Law and Journal* May: 377–408.

57   Davies (2002). *op. cit.*, p663.

58   Wray, L. R. (1998). *Understanding Modern Money: The Key to Full Employment and Price Stability*, Chapter 3. Cheltenham: Edward Elgar.

59   Wray (1998). *op. cit.* p. 43.

60   Grierson, P. (1977). *The Origins of Money*, London: Athlone Press, pp. 19–21.

61   Wikipedia (n.d.) Retrieved from http://en.wikipedia.org/wiki/Wergeld

62   Greirson (1977). *op. cit.* p. 43.

63   Innes (1913). *op. cit.*

64   Wray (1998). *op. cit.* Chapter 3.

65   Innes (1913). *op. cit.* p. 398.

66   Mosler, W. (2010). *Seven Deadly Innocent Frauds of Economic Policy.* Valance Co. Inc., p. 18.

67   Knapp, G. F. (1905). The State Theory of Money. London: Macmillan.

68   Febrero Eladio (2009). Three difficulties with neo-chartalism. *Journal of Post Keynesian Economics* (M.E. Sharpe, Inc.) 31(3): 523–541.

69   Innes (1913). *op. cit.*

70   Davies (2002). *op. cit.*, pp. 203–208 quoted in Ingham (2004) *op. cit.* p. 123.

71   Ferguson (2008). *op. cit.,* p. 31.

72   Carruthers, B. G. (1996). *City of Capital.* Princeton: Princeton University Press, p. 62.

73   Davies (2004). *op. cit.* p. 249.

74   *Ibid.* p. 251.

75   *Ibid.* p. 252.

76   Werner (2005). *op. cit.* Chapter 12.

77   Withers, H. (1909). *The Meaning of Money.* London, p. 20.

78   Rothbard, M. (1974). *The Case for a 100 Percent Gold Dollar.* Washington, DC: Libertarian Review Press; Huerta de Soto (2006/1998) *op. cit.*

79   Marx, K. (1894). Capital, volume III, part V. Chapter 29. Retrieved from http://www.marxists.org/archive/marx/works/1894-c3/ch29.htm [accessed 10 April 2011].

80   Werner (2005). *op. cit.* p.168.

81   El Diwany, T. (2003). *The Problem with Interest*, 2nd Edition. London: Kerotac, pp. 8–10.

82   Davies (2004). *op. cit.* p. 252.

83   Ferguson (2008). *op. cit.* pp. 165–118.

84   Ingham (2004). *op. cit.* p. 129.

85   Carruthers, B. G. (1996). *City of Capital*. Princeton: Princeton University Press, pp. 71–83.

86   Carruthers (1996). *op. cit.*

87   Ferguson (2008). *op. cit.* Chapter 2.

88   Pressnell, L.S. (1956). *Country Banking in the Industrial Revolution*. Oxford: University Press/Clarendon Press.

89   Davies (2005). *op. cit.* pp. 286–292.

90   *Ibid.* p. 311.

91   *Ibid.*

92   Retrieved from http://en.wikipedia.org/wiki/Bank_Charter_Act_1844

93   Bagehot, W. (1876). *Lombard Street: A Description of the Money Market*, New York: Scribner, Armstrong and Co., p. 25.

94   Davies records that country bank note issues ceased in 1921 when Lloyds absorbed Fox, Fowler and Co. of Wellington, Somerset with its 55 branches.

95   Werner (2005). *op. cit.* p. 179.

96   Cobbett, W. (1828). *Paper Against Gold*, p. 5, quoted in El Diwany (2003) *op. cit.*

97   Davies (2005). *op. cit.* p. 321.

98   Nichols (1992/1961). *op. cit.* p. 3.

99   Davies (2005). *op. cit.* p. 372.

100   Remarks by Governor Ben S. Bernanke at the H. Parker Willis Lecture in Economic Policy, Washington and Lee University, Lexington, Virginia, 2 March 2004.

101   Barry J. Eichengreen, B.J. (2008). *Globalizing capital: a history of the international monetary system.* Princeton University Press; 2nd edition, p. 82.

102   Eichengreen, B., Sachs, J. (1985). Exchange Rates and Economic Recovery in the 1930s. *Journal of Economic History* 45: 925–946.

103   Choudhri, E., Kochin, L.A. (1980). The Exchange Rate and the International Transmission of Business Cycle Disturbances: Some Evidence from the Great Depression. *Journal of Money, Credit, and Banking* 12: 565–574.

104   Davies, R., Richardson, P., Katinatire, V., (2010). Evolution of the UK Banking System. *Bank of England Quarterly Bulletin* 4: 321–332.

105   Croome, D. R., Johnson, G. J. (eds) (1970). *Money in Britain 1959–1969: The papers of the 'Radcliffe report – ten years after' conference at Hove, Sussex*, October 1969. London: Oxford University Press, p. 225.

106   Davies (2005) *op. cit.* p. 408.

107   Davies, R., Richardson, P. (2010). Evolution of the UK Banking System. *Bank of England Quarterly Bulletin* 4: 321–332. Retrievable from http://www.bankofengland.co.uk/publications/quarterlybulletin/qb1004.pdf

108   Davies, G. (2005). *op cit.* p. 409.

109   Monetary Policy Committee and Bank of England. (1999). 'The Transmission mechanism of monetary policy', *Bank of England*. Retrievable from www.bankofengland.co.uk

110   *Ibid.*

111   Pettifor (2006). *op. cit.* p. 62.

112   Werner (2005). *op. cit.*

113   Huber, J., Robertson, J. (2000). *Creating New Money: A Monetary reform for the information age*. London: **nef**.

114   ECB Europe. (2000). *op. cit.* p. 5.

115   For example, the Bank of England estimated notes and coins to be 3 per cent of money in circulation in 2007 – see Berry *et al.* (2007). *op. cit.* p. 377.

[116] Galbraith (1975). *op. cit.* p. 50.

[117] Dodd (1994). *op. cit.* pp. pxix-xxii.

[118] Harvey, D. (2006/1982). *The Limits of Capital.* London: Verso.

[119] Ingham (2004). *op. cit.*

[120] Dodd (1994). *op. cit.* p. xx.

[121] BIS. (2003). The role of central bank money in payments systems, Basel: Bank for International Settlements. Retrievable from http://www.bis.org/publ/cpss55.pdf

[122] Office of Fair Trading. (2008). *Personal Current Accounts in the UK,* p. 17. Retrievable from http://www.oft.gov.uk/shared_oft/reports/financial_products/OFT1005.pdf

[123] List of Reserve Scheme Participants. Retrievable from www.bankofengland.co.uk/markets/money/documentation

[124] Bank of England, *Payment Systems Oversight Report*, Retrievable from http://www.bankofengland.co.uk/publications/psor/index.htm

[125] Keynes J. M. (1930). *A Treatise on Money*, op. cit., Vol. 1, p26.

[126] Bank of England Annual Reports, 2000-2001 to 2008-2009. In each annual report, the Issue Department accounts state the amount payable to HM Treasury.

[127] Robertson, J., and Huber, J. (2000). *Creating New Money.* London: **nef**. Retreived from http://www.neweconomics.org/publications/creating-new-money

[128] *Ibid.* p80.

[129] *Ibid.* p.2; see also Appendix, table 4, footnote 3, p89.

[130] Ratio calculated by dividing M4 by Notes and Coins for December 2010.

[131] Bank of England statistics, M4 versus notes and coins 2006.

[132] Bank of England statistics, M4 versus Reserve Balances, 2010.

[133] Clews, R., Salmon, C., Weeken, O. (2010). The Bank's money market framework. *Bank of England Quarterly Bulletin* Q4: 292–301, p. 293.

[134] Clews *et al.* (2010). *op. cit.*

[135] *Ibid.* p. 295.

[136] *Financial Times* (2011, 5 August) Market Unimpressed by ECB action. Retrievable from http://www.ft.com/cms/s/0/fc04a956-bf71-11e0-898c-00144feabdc0.html#ixzz1ULKrwIT9 [accessed 6 August 2011].

[137] European central bank (2011, 7 August). Press release. para 6.

[138] Ingham (2004). *op. cit.* p.190.

[139] Davies (1994). *op cit.* p.663.

[140] United States Notes were also issued in significant proportions by the US government during the twentieth century. Werner (2005). *op. cit.* pp.258–259.

[141] Huber and Robertson (2000). *op. cit.*

[142] HM Government, Consolidated Fund Account 2009-2010, p. 2. Retrievable at www.official-documents.gov.uk/document/hc1011/hc04/0406/0406.pdf

[143] Adapted from presentation by Riddington, T. (2007). UK Government Accounts: The Exchequer Pyramid. London: DMO.

[144] Gilts are also issued to finance the redemption of maturing gilts.

[145] National Loans Fund Account 2009-2010. p.2.

[146] *Ibid.*

[147] Gilts come in fixed rate or variable rate forms, with the variable rate being linked to the Retail Price Index.

148   DMO. (2004). *A guide to the roles of the Debt Management Office and Primary Dealers in the UK Government bond market*. London: DMO, p.26, para 124.

149   *Ibid.* p.22, para 108.

150   National Audit Office. (2009). Government cash management. Appendices 2–8. Retrievable from http://www.nao.org.uk/publications/0809/cash_management.aspx

151   *Ibid.* p.14.

152   Werner (2005). *op. cit.*

153   *Ibid.*

154   HM Treasury. (March 2011). *UK Official holdings of international reserves*. London: HM Treasury. Retrievable from http://www.hm-treasury.gov.uk/d/pn_37_11.pdf

155   HM Treasury. *Exchange Equalisation Account: Report and Accounts 2009-10*. London: HM Treasury, para 6.

156   *Ibid.*, para 1.

157   *Ibid.*, p. 50, para 18.

158   *Ibid.*, para 54.

159   *Ibid.*, paras 2 and 3.

160   Letter to the Governor on the new Monetary Policy Framework, May 1997.

161   Bank of England. (Market Notice). Retrieved from http://www.bankofengland.co.uk/markets/reserves/marketnotice110228.pdf

162   Bank for International Settlements. (2010). *Triennial central bank Survey of Foreign Exchange and Over-The-Counter Interest Rate Derivatives Market Activity in April 2010. Report on global foreign exchange market activity in 2010*. BIS - Monetary and Economic Department, p.6.

163   With banks based in the United States accounting for 18 per cent, Japan 6 per cent, Singapore 5 per cent, Switzerland 5 per cent, Hong Kong SAR 5 per cent, and Australia 4 per cent .

164   Bank for International Settlements (2010). *op. cit.*

165   Hayek, F. (2008/1931). *Prices and Production*. Auburn, Alabama: Ludwig von Mises Institute, p. 289. Retrievable from http://mises.org/books/hayekcollection.pdf

166   See, for example, the list provided by Lord Turner, 'Reforming finance: are we being radical enough?', 2011 Clare Distinguished Lecture in Economics and Public Policy, Clare College, Cambridge, 18 February 2011.

167   Gorton, G., Metrick, A. (2010). *Regulating the shadow banking system*. London: Social Science Research Network.

168   Singh, M., Aitken, J. (2010). 'The (sizable) role of rehypothecation in the shadow banking system. *IMF working paper WP/10/172.*

169   Geithner, T. F. (June 2008). Reducing systemic risk in a dynamic financial system. Remarks at the Economic Club of New York, New York.

170   Gorton, G. and Metrick, A. (2009). 'Regulating the shadow banking system' NBER working paper 15223.

171   Werner, R.A. (2010a). Comment: Strengthening the Resilience of the Banking Sector, submission to the Basel Committee on Bank Supervision, April 2010. Retrievable from http://www.bis.org/publ/bcbs165/universityofsou.pdf

172   Werner, R.A. (2010b). A simple rule is needed to prevent future banking crises, Letter to the Editor, *Financial Times*, 17 November 2010.

173   Alessandri, P., and Haldane, A. G. (2009). Banking on the State, presentation delivered to the Federal Reserve Bank of Chicago twelfth annual International Banking Conference, p.26.

174   Jenkinson, N. (2008). *Strengthening Regimes for Controlling Liquidity Risk: Some Lessons from the Recent Turmoil*. Speech given at the Euromoney Conference on Liquidity and Funding Risk Managment, Hyatt Regency, London, 24 April 2008.

175   *Ibid.* p.7.

176   Clews *et al.* (2010). *op. cit.* p.297.

177   Voutsinas, K., Werner, R.A. (2011a). *New Evidence on the Effectiveness of Quantitative Easing in Japan.* Centre for Banking, Finance and Sustainable Development Discussion Paper. Southamption: University of Southampton, School of Management.

178   Lyonnet, V. (2011b). *Evidence on the Effectiveness of Quantitative Easing in the UK.* Centre for Banking, Finance and Sustainable Development Discussion Paper. Southamption: University of Southampton, School of Management.

179   Financial Services Authority. (2009, October) *PS09/16: Strengthening liquidity standards including feedback on CP08/22, CP09/13, CP09/14,* (para 6.27). Retrievable from http://www.fsa.gov.uk/pages/Library/Policy/Policy/2009/09_16.shtml .

180   *Financial Times.* (2011, 15 February). Liquidity gap yawns at new reserves clause. Retrievable from http://www.ft.com/cms/s/0/a75dbab2-385a-11e0-959c-00144feabdc0.html#axzz1MM2xlhBr.

181   Board of Governors of the Federal Reserve System. Retrievable from http://www.federalreserve.gov/monetarypolicy/reservereq.htm#text2 [accessed 9 August 2011].

182   As reported in the *Financial Times,* "Regulators poised to soften new bank rules", p17, September 6ᵗʰ 2011.

183   Goodhart, C.A.E. (1989). Has Moore become too horizontal? *Journal of Post-Keynesian Economics* 14: 134–136.

184   For an account of endogenous money: Parguez, A., Seccareccia, M. (2000). The credit theory of money: the monetary circuit approach. pp. 101–124, in Smithin (2000) *op. cit.*

185   Friedman, M. (1963). Inflation: Causes and Consequences. New York: Asia Publishing House.

186   Werner, R.A. (1995). Liquidity Watch report, Jardine Fleming Securities, Tokyo.

187   Werner, R.A. (2001, 2003). *Princes of the Yen, Japan's central bankers and the Transformation of the Economy.* New York: M. E. Sharpe.

188   Werner. (2005). *op. cit.*

189   Barro, R., Grossman, H. (1976). *Money, Employment and Inflation.* Cambridge: Cambridge University Press.

190   Mullbauer, J., Portes, R. (1978). Macroeconomic models with quantity rationing. *Economic Journal,* 88: 788–821.

191   Malinvaud, E. (1977). *The Theory of Unemployment Reconsidered,* Oxford: Basil Blackwell.

192   Werner (2005). *op. cit.* p.193.

193   *Ibid.*

194   Stiglitz, J. and Weiss, A. (1981). Credit rationing in markets with imperfect information. *American Economic Review,* 71: 393–410. Werner (2005). *op. cit.* p.193.

195   Stiglitz and Weiss (1981). *op. cit.*; see also Stigler, G. (1967). Imperfections in the Capital Market. *Journal of Political Economy,* June 1967, 85, 287-92.

196   Tucker (2008). *op. cit.* p 97.

197   Stiglitz and Weiss (1981). *op. cit.*

198   Blanchard, O., Fischer, I. (1989). Lectures on Macroeconomics, Cambridge, MA: MIT Press, p.479, quoted in Werner (2005) *op. cit.* p.193.

199   Werner, R.A. (1997). Towards a new monetary paradigm: A quantity theorem of disaggregated credit, with evidence from Japan. Kredit und Kapital Vol: 276–239.

200   Werner. (2005). *op. cit.*

201   Bank of England. (2011). *Trends in Lending.* Retrievable from http://www.bankofengland.co.uk/publications/other/monetary/trendsinlending2011.htm

202 Mullbauer, J., Portes, R. (1978). Macroeconomic models with quantity rationing. Economic Journal, 88: 788-821.

203 Werner (2005). *op. cit.* p.198.

204 World Bank. (1993). *The East Asian Miracle, Economic Growth and Public Policy*, Oxford: Oxford University Press.

205 Chen, Y., Werner, R.A. (2010). *The Monetary Transmission Mechanism in China.* Centre for Banking, Finance and Sustainable Development Discussion Paper. Southampton: School of Management, University of Southampton.

206 Werner (2003). *op. cit.*

207 Ingham, G. (2008). Capitalism. Cambridge: Polity Press, p.53.

208 Ingham. (2004). o*p. cit.* p. 128.

209 Thiel, V. (2009). *Doorstep Robbery*. London: **nef.**

210 Goodhart, C.A.E. (1975). Monetary Relationships: A View from Threadneedle Street. *Papers in Monetary Economics.* Location: Reserve Bank of Australia.

211 Leyshon and Thrift (1997). *op. cit.* p. 294.

212 Dodd (1994). *op. ci*t. p.xix.

213 Keynes (1930). *op. cit.*

214 Carruthers, B. G. (2005). The Sociology of Money and Credit. In Smelser, N. J., Swedberg, R. (eds). The Handbook of Economic Sociology, 2nd Edition, Princeton: Russell Sage Foundation.

215 Minsky, H. P. (2008/1986). Stabilizing an Unstable Economy. New York: McGraw Hill.

216 Knapp (1905). *op. cit.* p.45.

217 Ingham (2004). *op. cit.*

218 Keynes (1930). *op. cit.* p.3.

219 Mellor (2010). *op. cit.*

220 For more detailed formulae, see: Werner (2005). *op. cit.*

221 Reinhart, C. M., Rogoff, K, S. (2009). *This Time is Different: Eight Centuries of Financial Folly.* Princeton: Woodstock.

222 Werner, R.A. (2009). *Can credit unions create credit? An analytical evaluation of a potential obstacle to the growth of credit unions.* Discussion Paper Series, No. 2/09. Southampton: Centre for Banking, Finance and Sustainable Development, University of Southampton.

223 Werner, R.A. (2010). Comment: Range of Methodologies for Risk and Performance Alignment of Remuneration.Submission to the Basel Committee on Banking Supervision, 31 December 2010. Retrievable from http://www.bis.org/publ/bcbs178/richardwerner.pdf

224 The interest rate at which the London banks lend to each other is known as the London Interbank Offered Rate (LIBOR).

225 Clews *et al.* (2010). *op. cit.* pp.292–301.

226 Chart reproduced from speech by: Fisher (2011). *op. cit.*

227 Mac Gorain, S. (2005). Stabilising short-term interest rates, *Bank of England Quarterly Bulletin*, Q4: 2005

228 Tucker, P. (2004). Managing the central bank's balance sheet: where monetary policy meets financial stability. *Bank of England Quarterly Bulletin* **Q3***:* 364.

229 *Ibid.* p.367.

230 Chart reproduced from speech by: Fisher (2011). *op. cit.*

231   Bank for International Settlements. (2008). Committee on Payment and Settlement Systems .Progress in reducing foreign exchange settlement risk. BIS - Monetary and Economic Department, p.5.

232   Lindley, R. (2008). Reducing foreign exchange settlement risk. *BIS Quarterly Review* p.56.

233   A bank account that one bank holds for another bank is often called a 'nostro' account, and the bank holding the nostro account is often referred to as a nostro bank.

234   Bank for International Settlements. (2008). *BIS Quarterly Review.* p.55.

235   See endnote 9.

236   Bank for International Settlements. *Supervisory Guidance for Managing Settlement Risk in Foreign Exchange Transactions.,* BIS - Monetary and Economic Department, p.11.

237   CLS. (February 2011). *CLS market share report.* p.1.

238   Bank of England. (June 2003). *Strengthening financial infrastructure – Financial Stability Review. June 2003.* London: Bank of England, p. 81.

239   Bank of England. (March 2011). *Payment Systems Oversight Report 2010, March 2011.* London: Bank of England, p. 17.

240   Bank of England. (September 2009). *The Bank of England's oversight of interbank payment systems under the Banking Act 2009.* London: Bank of England, p. 8.

241   Lindley (2008). *op. cit.*

242   CLS Bank. (n.d.). About us. Retrieved from http://www.cls-group.com/Publications/CLS%20About%20Us.pdf

243   Bank for International Settlements. (2008). *Committee on Payment and Settlement Systems .Progress in reducing foreign exchange settlement risk.* Location: BIS – Monetary and Economic Department, p.23.

ABOUT THE AUTHORS

Josh Ryan-Collins is a Senior Researcher at **nef** (the new economics foundation) where he is leading a programme of research on the history and practice of monetary systems. He is studying for a PhD in finance and banking at the University of Southampton.

Tony Greenham is Head of Finance and Business at **nef**. He is a former investment banker, a Chartered Accountant and is a regular writer and media commentator on banking reform.

Professor Richard Werner is Director of the Centre for Banking, Finance and Sustainable Development at the University of Southampton and author of two best-selling books on banking and economics. He is credited with popularising the term 'quantitative easing' in 1994 whilst Chief Economist at Jardine Fleming Securities (Asia), following a spell as visiting research fellow at the Japanese Central Bank.

Andrew Jackson worked on the research for this book after graduating from the University of Sussex with an MSc in Development Economics.